Here at Last is Love

Drawing by Barry Moser

Praise for *Here at Last is Love*

"Father Hopkins wrote, 'This Jack, joke, poor potsherd, | patch, matchwood, immortal diamond, / Is immortal diamond.' Dunstan Thompson is an immortal diamond too long lost to poetry readers. Here are poems that show the workings of a complex interiority in touch with history's quirks, the world at war, personal relationships, and struggles of the human heart. Even at their most fervently erotic, they disclose a yearning for something that would allow the poems' various speakers to be more so that they may love more fully. From the elaborate sensuality of the early poems to the plainspoken urbanity and wit of the later, one constantly encounters an exuberance for life, a quest for meaning in a turbulent world, and openness to the divine spark in all things. This is a volume to be cherished, one that brings us back into touch with a vital American voice."

—Jerry Harp, author of *Creature*, *Gatherings*, and *Urban Flowers, Concrete Plains*

"This remarkable volume should complicate efforts to make a conversion narrative out of Thompson's poetry. Theological and erotic 'loneliness' in the early work are inextricable from and further enriched by an astonishing sensibility concerning war. What could belong more to Catholic tradition than poetry which joins contemplation, eroticism, and physical suffering? Without the critical constrictions of sexual identification, we can compare Thompson's formal poems to Millay's impassioned sonnets as well as to Crane's intricate music and metaphors. We are freed to consider breadth rather than trajectory: his insistent rhymes, striking meter, and haunting addresses that, in later works, move toward relaxed cadences, sublimated references, and less directly personal subjects. Lucky for us, we don't have to choose between binaries. Much gratitude to the editor for presenting the strongest of Thompson's work as a whole and highlighting for us its power and its revisionary place in modern poetics."

—Martha Serpas, author of *The Diener* and *The Dirty Side of the Storm*

"From the very beginning, with the 1943 publication of his volume *Poems* and his editorship of the influential Modernist literary magazine *Vice Versa*, Dunstan Thompson established himself as one of the most rigorous, formally adept, and brilliant poets of his generation. Here, for the first time, Gregory Wolfe draws poems from the poet's entire writing life, including his harrowing, erotic wartime poetry and his almost entirely unavailable, more reflective work of maturity. In doing so, he brings to new audiences the work of an essential mid-century poet, one I am confident will become much more important as his readership expands."

—Kevin Prufer, co-editor of *Dunstan Thompson: On the Life and Work of a Lost American Master*

"The bubble reputation is unreliable. Nearing the end, both Melville and Crane believed themselves forgotten. After Auden came to the United States and renewed the faith he had earlier put aside, much of his audience devalued his later poems. Dunstan Thompson's fame underwent a similar eclipse, an injustice this volume strives to remedy. The preface by Gregory Wolfe and afterword by Dana Gioia begin the task of locating and elucidating Thompson's excellence, both as a novice and a mature poet. His choice to be celibate in later life is one he likely would not make today, given that we now have support organizations for gay Catholics like Dignity. But that choice has no bearing on the value of his work, which exchanged the lushness and romantic difficulty of the early poems for a simpler and more vulnerable approach. Early and late, he enjoyed a skill with meter and rhyme that few twentieth-century poets have equaled."

—Alfred Corn, author of *Unions*

"Dunstan Thompson's poetry first became known to me in Oscar Williams' *The New Pocket Anthology of American Verse*, one of my English texts from high school. His lovely poems in that book—'Nor Mars His Sword,' 'The Lay of the Battle of Tombland'—were lost to me when I lost the anthology somewhere along the way. Now I am happy to see these poems restored, with much else of value, in this selection edited by Gregory Wolfe. *Here at Last is Love*, indeed, and here again is Dunstan Thompson, with a lyricism and a faith that remain rare in our poetry."

—Mark Jarman, author of *Bone Fires: New and Selected Poems*

"How often are we gifted with a collection of poems like Dunstan Thompson's, which have been uncovered and restored to life again by Gregory Wolfe and Dana Gioia? Thompson was an American poet (1918–1975) in a tradition that encompasses, among others, Hart Crane, T.S. Eliot, and W.H. Auden, and also includes the Greek and Roman classics in a fashion reminiscent of Robert Lowell. Thompson's early homoerotic poems—rising as they do from the fever and exhaustion of World War II—still have an amazing capacity to enchant and terrorize us. Add to that a Catholic vision which manages to embody the darkness of Baudelaire's flowers of evil as well as the hard-won redemptive vision of Augustine, John of the Cross, and Hopkins, and you have a sense of what Thompson has to offer us. This volume is a truly significant addition to twentieth-century American poetry and, even more, a vivid, heartbreaking, and authentic contribution to the core poetry of the Catholic imagination."

—Paul Mariani, author of *Epitaphs for the Journey: New, Selected, and Revised Poems*

Here at Last is Love

SELECTED POEMS OF

DUNSTAN THOMPSON

EDITED BY Gregory Wolfe

WITH AN AFTERWORD BY Dana Gioia

SL/.NT

BOOKS

Slant Books
P.O. Box 60295
Seattle, WA 98160

www.slantbooks.com

HARDCOVER ISBN: 978-1-63982-013-9
PAPERBACK ISBN: 978-1-63982-012-2
EBOOK ISBN: 978-1-63982-014-6

Cataloging-in-Publication data:

Thompson, Dunstan, 1918–1975.

Here at last is love : selected poems of Dunstan Thompson / Dunstan Thompson ; edited with an introduction by Gregory Wolfe ; afterword by Dana Gioia.

HARDCOVER ISBN: 978-1-63982-013-9 | PAPERBACK ISBN: 978-1-63982-012-2 | EBOOK ISBN: 978-1-63982-014-6

xxxii + 128 p., 23 cm

1. American Poe y—21st Century. I. Wolfe, Gregory. II. Gioia, Dana. III. Title.

PS 3539.H65 H4 2015

Manufactured in the USA.

Table of Contents

Introduction

GREGORY WOLFE

In place of gold, he sets
    A banished life between
Driftwood, and out of fish nets
    Roofs his loss with sea green.

Thus lives unexiled, though
    Abandoned, stranded, scanned
By the Dog Star only, for so
    Based, his poems are his own land.

—DUNSTAN THOMPSON, "Ovid on the Dacian Coast"

Until quite recently, the life and work of the mid-twentieth century American poet Dunstan Thompson were known only to a dwindling number of literary historians and aging contemporaries. For those few who were acquainted with his story, the narrative had a familiar—even comforting—shape: it was a tragic tale of "rise and fall." There was Thompson's rise to prominence in the Anglo-American literary world during the 1940s, followed by his equally sudden disappearance from the scene.

Thanks to the efforts of his longtime partner and literary executor, Philip Trower, and the investigations of a few literary sleuths, a much more complete and nuanced version of Thompson's story has begun to emerge, leading many of the poets and critics who have rediscovered him to hail Thompson as a lost and unsung American master.

At the same time—even in the early days of this revival—Thompson's biography and poetry have generated controversy, as will become clear. Among his current admirers there has been a tendency to claim him in the name of a larger cause or worldview. But it is to be hoped that the publication of this book will temper the debate over—and deepen the appreciation of—Thompson's *oeuvre* by offering a fuller account of his life and gathering much of his best work written over the course of four decades.

Encountered in a single volume, these poems demonstrate that while there are clear differences in style and subject matter between the two major phases of Thompson's writing life, there are also unities of theme and expression that have yet to be fully grasped and valued. In William Blake's beautiful image, there is a "golden string" winding through Thompson's poetry that is worth tracing.

> I give you the end of a golden string,
>   Only wind it into a ball:
> It will lead you in at Heaven's gate,
>   Built in Jerusalem's wall....

Finding that golden string will require a revision of the received wisdom. The sketchy version of Thompson's story—the one that has lodged in the minds of the few who have even heard of him—begins with Thompson as a young poet who made his mark at Harvard University in the late 1930s and the New York literary scene in the early 1940s. The next chapter recounts the publication of two volumes of highly acclaimed "baroque" poetry that explore both the experience of World War II and the complex emotional territory of homosexual desire. In the words of poet Edward Field, he and others of his generation considered Thompson one of the rising "stars of modern poetry," worthy of comparison to Hart Crane, W.H. Auden, Stephen Spender, and Dylan Thomas. Then, without warning—so the story goes—Thompson, who had been a lively fixture in the literary circles of both New York and London, disappeared from the scene. There were rumors that he had reverted to the Catholic faith of his youth, renounced his gay identity, and gone to live as a recluse in rural England, never to be heard from again.

The epilogue to the tale was added when a collection of his later poetry—*Poems: 1950–1974*—was published posthumously.[1] The collection provided evidence not only that Thompson had returned to Catholic faith and practice, but wrote insipid devotional poetry that abandoned the flamboyant style of his youth for a wan, bookish classicism. Just as Robert Browning lamented William Wordsworth's turn from youthful radicalism to a more conservative vision in the poem "The Lost Leader," so Thompson has been characterized as a self-hating homosexual who embraced a faith that suppressed his true identity and genius.

Alongside this version of the narrative lies its inverted mirror image, espoused by Catholic and other religious readers who have hailed Thompson as a champion of the true faith who rejected a hateful way of life and utterly self-absorbed, decadently romantic poetry for a noble austerity of style and vision.

Like all such pieces of received wisdom, these parallel versions of the narrative I have recounted are caricatures, ones that perhaps few hold in such extreme forms. But in the absence of more available information about Thompson's life and ready access to his poetry, these and other two-dimensional accounts have left a strong impression. This can readily be seen in the recently published book *Dunstan Thompson: On the Life and Work of a Lost American Master*, edited by D.A. Powell and Kevin Prufer. The editors demonstrate a gracious desire for inclusion by publishing essays from the entire spectrum of opinion about Thompson—noting, however, that the result is a "cacophony."

No doubt that cacophony will continue, but in making the best of Thompson's poetry from all periods of his life available in a single volume, it may be possible for readers of every persuasion to detect the glint of a golden string that runs through this newly restored tapestry.

Terry Dunstan Thompson was born on August 30, 1918, at Lawrence and Memorial Hospital in New London, Connecticut.[2] His background has been called "patrician," but that is misleading on several levels. Certainly there was some wealth in the family on his mother's side, and professional and literary distinction on his father's side, but his immediate family had limited means, and Thompson's relationship to exalted social circles was marginal at best.

His paternal grandfather, Charles T. Thompson, spent most of his career on the staff of the Associated Press, rising to chief of the Paris and Washington, D.C., bureaus. Among Charles's crowning achievements was detailed reporting from the Italian front during World War I, including the retreat from Caporetto (an episode made famous by Ernest Hemingway's *A Farewell to Arms*), which he later chronicled in book form. For his reporting, the French government made him a Chevalier of the Legion of Honor, and the Italian Army gave him a decoration. A sophisticated man of the world, Charles was something of a *bon vivant*, equally at home in news rooms and casinos.

Charles's wife, Flora McDonald, was also a journalist and writer. According to Trower, she was more of an intellectual than her husband. Flora wrote both political tracts (one of which elicited a response from pioneering feminist Elizabeth Cady Stanton) and fiction. At one point she was asked to write a book attacking the Catholic Church, but in the course of her research she was won over by her supposed enemy and received into the church. Charles, too, became a Catholic, though whether before or after his wife is not known. The marriage eventually became strained and the couple lived apart. Flora spent her later years in Washington, D.C., where she became the hostess of a salon for Catholic clergy and cultured lay people. Though he may have been too young to experience this salon, Dunstan would certainly have inherited an awareness of Catholicism as a living tradition, capable of generating serious intellectual thought and dialogue.

Thompson's father, Terry Brewster Thompson, was one of Charles and Flora's three children. Thanks to Charles's job, the family lived in the town of Giverny, near Monet, but to Thompson's regret, his father could remember little of the painter other than catching glimpses of him at work *en plein air*. Terry attended schools in France and England, where he seems to have imbibed a highly traditional sense of moral rectitude and public duty.

One of the few family stories that survives about Charles—and which provides some insight into the differences between father and son—is that when he was asked to look after his grandson Dunstan, he ended up taking him to a casino, where the child found much to amuse himself. Thompson's father was likely not amused.

Indeed, there is some evidence that Terry reacted against his father's worldly, cosmopolitan way of life. He chose a more regimented life as a career naval officer, specializing in naval engineering, and his Catholic spirituality has been described by Trower in his unpublished memoir of Thompson as "French Cistercian"—referring to the austere order of reformed Benedictine monks.

Thompson's mother, Virginia Leita Montgomery, came from a wealthy Catholic family that had its roots in Louisiana but became well established in Washington, D.C. Through her mother, Leita was related to the Carrolls and Lees, pioneering Catholic immigrant families who had arrived in Maryland in the late seventeenth century. Charles Carroll was the only Catholic signer of the Declaration of Independence. His cousin Daniel Carroll was a signer of the U.S. Constitution.

According to Trower, Thompson's mother "was shy, devout, innocent, and unworldly in a way now difficult to imagine." He continues: "his mother unwittingly imbued him with many of her fears and anxieties as well as her shyness and nervousness.... When I think of Dunstan and his mother together I see, not so much a mother and child, as two children deeply entwined emotionally, struggling to cope with the adult world, and with the younger child often having to take the initiative."

Leita experienced a number of miscarriages before and after the birth of her son. Sensing that she would not be able to bring another child to term, Thompson's parents adopted a girl named Betty when he was about seven years old. Given their difference in age and Thompson's eventual boarding school education, brother and sister never became close. In Trower's words, Thompson's experience growing up was closer to that of an only child.

The member of his mother's family who would prove most influential in Thompson's life was his great-aunt Leita, who had married the second Catholic chief justice of the U.S. Supreme Court, Edward Douglass White. In contrast to Thompson's mother, Trower describes his great-aunt, known throughout the family as "Aunt Leita," as a stable, sensible woman. She took a shine to young Dunstan, and when she died in 1934 left a legacy to him that would enable him to live and work as a poet throughout his life without having to hold a job.

Thompson's childhood followed a pattern of sorts. The family moved whenever his father shifted to a new naval base, and then Terry would be gone on long deployments, leaving the boy to grow extremely close to—and protective of—his mother. There is no evidence that Thompson feared his father or had a fraught relationship with him, other than anecdotes arising out of typical adolescent arguments (for example, over the consumption of alcohol). Still, even in Trower's lengthy memoir of Thompson, the father remains a rather distant, nebulous figure.

One constant in Thompson's childhood was the liturgical life of the Catholic Church. A commentator has made much of the family having ties to various Catholic dignitaries, including cardinals and archbishops, but for Thompson the experience of faith had less to do with high-ranking clerical friends of the family than with the sacramental life of the church. From a young age Thompson was an altar boy, often getting up early in the morning to serve at the first Mass of the day. In stark contrast to Thompson's father's "French

Cistercian" sensibility, Trower calls his mother's faith "highly color-ful and Italianate," an element of Leita's disposition the son seems to have shared.

Another formative experience was foreign travel, something that came naturally to Thompson's father, given his naval career and European upbringing. There were trips to places like Panama, Eng-land, France, Belgium, and Germany (where the family attended the Passion Play at Oberammergau and visited the Catholic mystic Therese Neumann, who experienced the stigmata, the wounds of Christ's Passion, in her flesh). On a trip to Rome they had an audi-ence with Pope Pius XI, who gave them one of his white silk skull caps.

When he was twelve, Thompson was sent to Georgetown Prep in Washington, D.C., at first as a day student but then as a boarder. Perhaps sensing that his long deployments had left too much dis-tance between himself and his son, Terry brought him out to Vil-lanova Prep in the Ojai Valley when he was stationed in California, but then left on another long deployment.

It was at yet another Catholic school—Canterbury School in New Milford, Connecticut, which he attended for most of his high school years—that Thompson's literary abilities began to be no-ticed. One of his teachers, Jimmy Doyle, encouraged him to write poetry. And despite what he would later call his "shyness from my youth," Thompson also began to demonstrate a genius for friend-ship at Canterbury. In fact, Thompson stayed in touch with a num-ber of his Canterbury teachers and classmates for many years, some to the very end of his life.

When it came to the choice of which college or university Thompson should attend, there was some discussion within the fam-ily. In those days most Catholics were expected to send their children to Catholic institutions such as Georgetown, Notre Dame, or Bos-ton College, but Thompson's uncle Frederick had long championed Harvard as the pinnacle of higher education in America. And so, be-ing the faithful Catholic family they were, ecclesiastical dispensation was sought for and granted so Thompson could attend Harvard.

By all accounts, Thompson flourished at Harvard in many ways. He gravitated quickly to the faculty who were also poets, especially Robert Davis, Theodore Spencer, and Robert Hillyer. The latter, a High Anglican with a decidedly traditionalist preference for form and romantic diction, was to have the most lasting influence on Thompson. Many years later, in a tribute to Hillyer, Thompson would call him a "gonfalonier of 'Reaction,'" a critic of Modernists like Eliot and Pound who championed the "gentlemanly" verse of the sixteenth and late nineteenth centuries.[3]

Equally important were his close friendships with some of the most gifted writers among his Harvard classmates. Two of the most important and longest-lasting were with Harry Brown and Billy Abrahams. Brown, who would go on to write a World War II novel, *A Walk in the Sun*, which was made into a film starring Dana Andrews, ended up as a Hollywood screenwriter. But in his Harvard years Brown was immersed in literature and poetry. Trower describes Brown as temperamentally the opposite of Thompson, a "typical man's man, as practical as Dunstan was impractical."

Abrahams was more like Thompson on a number of levels. Both had a homosexual orientation and valued literary conversation, wit, and repartee. They were "romantic over a rock-bed of realism… brothers in a savage world," in Trower's words. Abrahams would eventually have a distinguished career as an editor and publisher. During their Harvard years they would have only one significant falling-out: when Abrahams tried to enlist Thompson's support for the cause of the Republicans in the Spanish Civil War. Whether because of his Catholic background or an innate sense of moderation in political matters, Thompson disappointed Abrahams when he expressed ambivalence about that cause.

Thompson's extracurricular activities centered on *The Harvard Monthly*, a campus magazine originally founded by George Santayana and others that had gone defunct and only just been revived when Thompson arrived at Harvard. He served as contributor, editorial board member, and, eventually, as editor. Among the poems he contributed was "To Hart Crane," whose poetry had already exerted considerable influence on him.

Thompson's *Monthly* essay contributions also revealed a satirical and contrarian streak that would manifest itself in various ways throughout his life and literary career. They included a *jeu d'esprit* imagining communists taking over Harvard, a piece mocking Isabella Stewart Gardner (the eccentric Boston socialite and patron of the arts), and "Ants on the Ash Heap," an attack on the Harvard English department that spared only Robert Hillyer.

The one *Monthly* piece that caused the greatest stink was "Fragrant Futility," a send-up of the Cowley Fathers, a monastic order within the Episcopal Church. Thompson had visited the monastery in Boston with seemingly benign intentions and was received graciously, but the essay, according to a memoir by his classmate Sanford Gifford, "made fun of their High-Church efforts to be more Catholic than their Episcopal denomination." As Gifford writes, Thompson's "own Catholic background made him the perfect critic,"[4] but the essay infuriated Hillyer, who forced the young satirist to apologize to the good Fathers.

While his Catholic identity might have provided Thompson with the proper satirical angle for his essay, it is clear that he had lost his faith at some point late in high school or soon after arriving at Harvard. There seems little doubt that this loss of faith coincided with the beginning of his liaisons with men. As the poet Katie Ford notes: "It seems that it was not a crisis of faith that drove Thompson into a 'lapsed' period of Catholic practice. Perhaps sexual and social, what was forbidden created a crisis of desire, not of belief."[5] Trower adds that Thompson's memory of the period was of living in an anguished limbo: he attempted to play the fashionable skeptic, but retained an instinctive sense that belief was vital to human flourishing. And yet he could not embrace the only two grand belief systems that seemed open to him in the late thirties: Catholicism and Marxism.

Perhaps this underlying turmoil contributed to Thompson's academic troubles, for despite his brilliant literary achievements at the *Monthly*, he regularly failed to attend classes and pass examinations. To the surprise of his peers, he dropped out of Harvard in 1939 after his third year, a move that Trower believes was intended to forestall expulsion.

Rather than sink into depression and lethargy, Thompson traveled. He had already been going on trips abroad the previous summers, including visits to Ireland, England, and Mexico. In the summer of 1938, he had spent a month in England studying with the poet Conrad Aiken, who was considered a major writer at the time. He returned in the summer of 1939 to spend another month with Aiken, who gave him a personal introduction to T.S. Eliot. Writing to a friend, Aiken described Thompson as the "cleverest" of his students, "a great rattler and improviser, a real gift of the gab, raconteur, mimic, clown, somewhat in a hurry but shrewd too, adaptable and imitative...but honest and psychologically alert."[6]

After this trip, Thompson established himself in New York City—effortlessly, it would appear. His connections and literary gifts quickly placed him in the center of the city's cultural life. He befriended many of the leading lights of the period, including George Barker, Horace Gregory, Marya Zaturenska, and the eminent critic and editor Malcolm Cowley. One of the most valuable connections he made was with Oscar Williams, the editor of widely read poetry anthologies—being included in those volumes gave Thompson's work valuable exposure.

Beyond writing and publishing his own poetry, Thompson's most ambitious project during this time was the founding, with his Harvard friend Harry Brown, of a "little journal" devoted strictly to contemporary poetry, called *Vice Versa*. It "exuded the austere and practical tone of a reformist enterprise," according to poet and critic Dana Gioia, who also notes the "mordant humor and youthful high spirits" that were on a par with *The Harvard Monthly*.[7] Setting the tone of *Vice Versa* were its slash-and-burn reviews, which gleefully took down luminaries like E.E. Cummings, Wallace Stevens, and W.H. Auden. But at the same time, Brown and Thompson were able to publish original poetry by the likes of Auden, Dylan Thomas, Ezra Pound, Weldon Kees, Edith Sitwell, and George Barker.

Vice Versa was funded by Thompson himself, but in spite of the legacy he was now receiving from his aunt Leita's estate, the money wasn't sufficient to cover all the printing bills and other costs associated with the magazine. Then came Pearl Harbor, and it became clear that *Vice Versa* would have to cease publication after three issues.

Everything was about to change.

Many years after the war, Thompson wrote to a friend: "I had a gallant war record—carrying Coca-Cola bottles to sergeants, and writing the Colonel's letters to his friends back home. I used to mess up the grammar afterwards to make it sound more authentic." He adds that he really shouldn't make fun since the officer in question had been quite kind to him. The humor here is not that much of an exaggeration in some ways, since none of his wartime assignments brought him near combat and most were tedious. He eventually ended up working for the Office of War Information in London, the branch of the war effort responsible for both information and propaganda. While his role there might have drawn upon some of Thompson's literary skills, the experience could not have been that interesting, since in the many years he and Philip Trower spent together after the war Thompson never found anything worth recounting about that job.

At the same time, the stresses and strains of the war—and some of its horrors—were never fully absent from his experience. In particular, he was present in London for much of the Blitz and impressed more than one friend with his fearlessness during bombing raids. A couple of his friends were working in London, which helped to break up the tedium between bombings. Throughout these years he continued to have furtive, short-lived sexual relationships with other men, including many in the military—but never with anyone who might be considered one of his close friends. The pattern of these encounters can be traced in his early poetry: brief, intense infatuations followed by a sense of indifference or betrayal, whether on his part of that of his partners.

He must have been buoyed by the publication of his first collection, simply entitled *Poems*, in 1943 by Simon & Schuster. The reviews were mixed, but where some saw "selfish egotism" and poems full of "private symbols," others praised the poems' "dash and splendor" and the "living, speaking voice of youth enmeshed in war." One critic who panned the collection nonetheless held that "the violence of his vision of the inner world, compounded of war, death, incertitude, isolation, reflects the cataclysm which traditional modes of thought and feeling are undergoing in the world today."[8]

After his demobilization in December 1945, Thompson returned to New York, where his reputation had grown. But even as he prepared a second collection of poems, which would appear as *Lament for the Sleepwalker* (1947), he had to contemplate what his post-war adult life would look like. He set himself up at the Algonquin Hotel and was often seen with friends and acquaintances and a martini in hand. But there were signs that he was going through some internal strife. One of his best friends, Howard Turner, wrote that during this period Thompson was "nervous, sometimes intemperate, argumentative—I came to feel wary in his presence, unsure of his moods, wondering where he was headed."

He decided that he would do what successful authors did: propose a book and get an advance from a publisher to live on for a time. He'd conceived the idea some time back of traveling to the Middle East and writing a book of reflections about it. Thanks to the efforts of Margot Johnson, his literary agent, Dodd, Mead and Company agreed to publish the book, and he traveled to Cairo in 1946.

There he reunited with someone he had met in London in early 1945, Philip Trower, to whom he had been introduced by a mutual friend. Trower was serving in Cairo in a branch of the

British Foreign Office known as the Political Intelligence Department. After a couple of American diplomats vacated Trower's Cairo apartment, Thompson moved in. This was the beginning of a relationship that would continue without interruption for the better part of three decades.

Five years younger than Thompson, Trower had been educated at Eton and then completed a war-shortened BA in history at Oxford University. He joined the army in 1942 but was wounded at the battle for the Anzio bridgehead in Italy and returned to England to recuperate. His army service obligation was for five years, which his work in Cairo enabled him to complete.

In Trower Thompson not only found an admirer and a lover, but also someone of fierce loyalty and great kindness. It was to become the first and only stable, long-term relationship that Thompson would ever experience. Though he was the younger man, Trower had an education equal to that of Thompson and his own literary and intellectual ambitions. They were well matched.

Thompson's experiences in the Middle East were rich and varied, but the book that came out of the six months he spent there, *The Phoenix in the Desert*, not published until 1951, was really more of a collection of sketches and impressions than a serious inquiry into the history, culture, and politics of the region. In the same way, his one published novel, *The Dove with the Bough of Olive* (1954), would not catch fire with readers. Drawing on the satirical fiction of writers like Evelyn Waugh and Ivy Compton-Burnett, it was made up primarily of conversations rather than extended description, character development, or attention to plot. The limited success of his two prose books would provide no incentive for him to abandon poetry.

When they returned to London in early 1947, Thompson and Trower found a flat together, but it wasn't long before they realized that Thompson's inheritance didn't leave much left over after the expensive city rent. Trower, who had once intended to pursue a career in law, had decided to try his own luck as a full-time writer.

So he contacted a cousin who found an inexpensive house for let on the northern coast of Norfolk in the village of Cley next the Sea. Neither Thompson nor Trower imagined at the time that their sojourn to Norfolk would be anything but temporary. But they were to remain there until Thompson's death in 1975.

Given the course of Thompson's literary fortunes from this point forward, and his eventual return to his Catholic faith in 1952, it has been tempting for some to conclude that he made some sort of conscious decision to become a recluse. This was not his intention. Travel to London, even by car, was a long and tiring journey, but right up until their move Thompson and Trower had continued to meet socially with the likes of T.S. Eliot, Stephen Spender, Cyril Connolly, Rose Macaulay, Laurie Lee, Roy Fuller, and many others, indicating the opposite of a desire for retreat. At the same time, it is also true that to some extent, they simply moved into a more settled phase of life together.

There were other signs, however subtle, that Thompson was settling into himself. The poems at the end of *Lament for the Sleep-walker*, for example, show a dramatic shift from self-preoccupation to a focus outside his immediate experience. Not only that, but there is also a clear move toward simplified diction and direct syntax. In the moving "Sonnets to My Father," written after his father's death in 1945, Thompson's lines have gone from "baroque" to "austere":

> Ah, Captain, you died at peace, although a war
> Broke your heart, as once before your son had.
> The years like roses darken, die: so fade
> The roses on your grave. How the dead are
> Easily put by. How the incomparable dead
> Are easily forgotten. How still the dead.

Similarly, in "This Life, This Death," the speaker of the poem surveys the various fears and temptations that assail him in his loneliness, yet concludes:

> This life, this death, to be met with everywhere,
> I know now to be my good hope and not despair.

In "The Moment of the Rose," a title that seems a deliberate reference to the line "The moment of the rose and the moment of the yew-tree / Are of equal duration" in Eliot's *Four Quartets*, the poet can say:

> The end of love is that the heart is still
> As the rose no wind distresses, still as light
> On the unmoved grass, or as the humming bird
> Poised the pure moment by an act of will.

Knowing as he does now the experience of human friendship "my childhood promised me," quietly acknowledged in the next stanza, the poet not only finds peace but also the capacity to act. The phrase "act of will" seems an almost unconscious borrowing from traditional Catholic theology. St. Augustine famously equated will with love: "*Amor meus, pondus meum*"—my love is my weight. When we will something, it is because we love it. Whether Thompson knew the quotation or not, there is also an echo here of Kierkegaard's "purity of heart is to will one thing."

The exact sequence of events that led to Thompson's return to Catholic faith and practice is uncertain. From various accounts, including letters he wrote to others about it, it is clear that at some point he began to say the rosary again. He also purchased the contemporary translation of the Gospels by Monsignor Ronald Knox, himself a well-known convert to Catholicism.

In a letter written later in his life Thompson recalls being in London in the mid-1940s, needing to get from Grosvenor Square to Berkeley Square, when he decides to take something of a "short cut" through the Jesuit Church of the Immaculate Conception, commonly known as Farm Street Church. There he witnesses an elderly priest rocking back and forth in the pulpit as he preaches to the congregation on the topic of love. As Thompson leaves the church he takes note of the priest's name, should he ever need to contact one.

There were also liturgical events that Thompson felt drawn to. Living as they did on the north Norfolk coast, he and Trower were only seven miles from Walsingham, England's oldest shrine to the Virgin Mary. One day the two of them bicycled there to witness a procession of pilgrims from all over Britain and France. Representatives from various communities and sodalities carried large white crosses. When a priest carrying a monstrance passed by—a highly ornate object with a consecrated host contained between glass panes within a golden sunburst pattern—Thompson knelt before it, as Catholics are expected to do.

He also proposed to Trower a more ambitious trip to Rome in 1950 for the Jubilee—a special holy year devoted to pardon and the remission of sins (a tradition with roots going back to Judaism). Specifically, Thompson wanted to witness the proclamation made *ex cathedra* by the Pope confirming the Assumption of the Blessed Virgin, the dogma asserting that the Virgin Mary was "assumed," body and soul, into heaven, without experiencing death as we know it. They got tickets that put them atop Bernini's colonnade for the ceremony.

The trip wasn't all given over to piety, however. One night they attended a party at the Villa Aurelia where they saw Leonard Bernstein and Alberto Moravia. Thompson spent the evening talking about literature with Robert Lowell while Trower danced the night away with Lowell's wife, Elizabeth Hardwick.

They then went on to Assisi, Ravenna, and Venice. Trower would later reflect that the addition of Assisi to the itinerary should have signaled more clearly to him Thompson's movement back toward faith.

It wasn't until two years later—late summer or autumn of 1952—that Thompson told Trower that he intended to go to London to the priest he had heard at Farm Street Church to make his confession and return to the practice of the faith: "If he took this step, Dunstan explained before he set out for London, the nature of our relationship would have to change. We should have to live chastely. It is also possible he would be told we could no longer live together. Was I prepared for this. I said Yes."

Though Trower goes on to explain that he had had his own misgivings about their way of life, it is hard not to admire the generosity and selflessness of his response. Six months later, Trower was himself received into the Catholic Church. The question about whether they would be allowed to continue to live together was resolved in an unusual manner, given the assumptions many of us would make about the pre-Vatican II church. It was decided that they would, indeed, be allowed to stay together on the grounds that the strength of their love for one another would enable them to live chastely.

Needless to say, the subject of turning away from homosexual practice in the context of a religious conversion is a controversial one today. What should simply be noted here is that some of the conjectures that might be made about this experience in Thompson's life were not operative, for instance that a lack of intimacy due to age or some traumatic breakup might have caused the change. In 1952 Thompson was only thirty-four, and he made his decision seven years into what had become a stable, loving relationship.

From Thompson's perspective, at least, he would most likely have embraced the notion that he had in fact experienced, to use Katie Ford's words again, "a crisis of desire" rather than "a crisis of belief." But this particular crisis he felt as a call to re-order his desire toward the infinite rather than the finite, according to the teachings of the church he had always loved. What cannot be disputed is that the choice brought him joy, relief, and peace.

The debate that is likely to be more heated and long-lasting is the one about the quality of his later poetry. That Thompson continued to write and to have his literary agent represent him is not in question. Margot Johnson continued to send out both poems and entire collections that Thompson had put together, but they found no takers. After *Lament* was released, a few poems were printed in the multilingual journal *Botteghe Oscure*. Then, years later, "Images and Reflections" (his tribute to T.S. Eliot upon his reception of the Nobel Prize) was published in the *Paris Review* in 1963, while "Ovid on the Dacian Coast" appeared in the *New Yorker* in 1965.

No doubt there were many factors at play when it came to Thompson's failure to find publishers willing to take on his work. While not a recluse per se, he certainly did not keep up with literary circles as he once had. Then there was the shift in his style: known for writing in his self-revealing, baroque manner, the plainer style and greater reticence of the later poetry didn't fit the picture many had formed of his literary genius. This was the period, after all, of the emergence of Confessional poetry. Thompson's subject matter had also changed: much of it focused on history, culture, and memories of the places where he had grown up or traveled to.

In "Ovid on the Dacian Coast," Thompson imagined himself into the experience of the Roman poet, who had been exiled to a remote fringe of the Roman Empire while still at the height of his literary powers.

> The marsh birds wheel and shriek
>   Above him, as he takes
> Word after word from their bleak
>   Coast of love: his heart breaks.

The tone here is not one of anger or resentment but of elegiac melancholy as the poet seeks to "translate" the stones on the bleak coast into words and poems that become "his own land."

Thompson also composed quite a few poems with religious subjects, though they constitute perhaps only a third of his later work. These have come in for some sharp criticism. For example, Ford has argued against their merits on the basis that there is a clear distinction to be made between poetry, which depends on language that is surprising, and liturgy, which she contends is a communal language in which the surprise is felt within the believer rather than in the language itself.[9]

But this seems an odd way to construe the relationship between poetry and liturgy, given the long tradition in Western literature running from Dante and the Metaphysicals through Emily Dickinson and T.S. Eliot that hums with the resonance between these two forms of speech. Even in a brief, simple poem like "Fragment for Christmas," Thompson's capacity for wordplay and multiple levels of meaning is evident:

> Dear Lord, and only ever faithful friend,
> For love of us rejected, tortured, torn—
> And we were there; who on the third day rose
> Again, and still looks after us; descend
> Into each wrecked unstable house; be born
> In us, a Child among Your former foes.

The abruptness of "And we were there" suddenly implicates the reader in both the Passion and the Nativity of Christ (a pairing that goes back centuries in the theology and art of the church)—the way a dynamic baroque painting or sculpture can break the invisible plane between artist and viewer. "Wrecked unstable house" comes with its own set of surprises. Our homes are wrecked not only because they are broken by sin but also "recked" in that they are reckoned by God's perduring love. Those homes are also not only "unstable" in an emotional sense but are in a state far from the simplicity and purity of the stable into which the Son of God was born.[10]

That Thompson suffered from his inability to be published is attested to by Philip Trower. At one point he had hoped that T.S. Eliot might be interested in publishing him through Faber & Faber, but it came to nothing. Still, it would be wrong to assume that the melancholy Thompson felt about his literary fate left him depressed or paralyzed. Indeed, he continued writing poetry until the end.

The last two decades of his life were spent almost entirely in Cley. For someone who had traveled as much as he had, this might seem evidence of withdrawal, but for much of the 1950s he was actually embroiled in a legal wrangle with a contractor who had vastly overcharged for work done on one of the Georgetown town-houses in Washington, D.C., that constituted the source of his income. Then, by the 1960s, his health began to deteriorate.

For many years, the Marian shrine at Walsingham was a focal point—socially and spiritually—for Thompson and Trower, who frequently served at the altar. There were also trips to the nearby towns of Norfolk and Cambridge and, less frequently, to London. A steady stream of visitors—British and American—came to Cley. Thompson's Harvard friend Billy Abrahams came for many visits along with his partner, the writer Peter Stansky. Bishops, priests, seminarians, and other church friends were also among the regulars. Even when there were no visitors, the two men would faithfully observe happy hour, which consisted of gin and tonics and animated conversation.

Thompson's health began a rapid decline in the mid-1970s, and he finally became bedridden. According to Trower, he had been reluctant to see doctors but eventually did see a specialist who in December of 1974 diagnosed liver cancer. Only a few weeks earlier he had written a small poetic fragment that reads: "How small / everyone looks / in the great hall / of death."

Once during this period when Thompson became short-tempered with Trower, he later apologized: "It's my past sins coming out." About a week before he died he told Trower, "I'm so blessed. I've had a lot of discomfort, but no great pain."

The end came on January 19, 1975. Thompson was attended by his parish priest, who gave him the last rites. His gravestone bears the inscription: "O Crux ave, spes unica," a quotation thought to be from the sixth-century hymn, "Vexilla Regis Prodeunt," translated: "O hail the cross, our only hope." Trower recalls that at the burial there was a violent wind. "If it had been the funeral of anyone else, anyone who had a life like his own, [Thompson] would have said: 'Someone is furious. He has been defeated.'"

There is a moment late in Evelyn Waugh's novel *Brideshead Revisited* when the protagonist, Charles Ryder, encounters Cordelia Flyte, the youngest daughter of the Catholic family he had known and loved years earlier. When Ryder first met her she was a vivacious, mischievous child. But when he sees her again after many years she has grown into a plain woman, devoting her time to working with an ambulance service in World War II. "Tell me, Charles," she says. "When you first met me last night, did you think 'Poor Cordelia. Such an engaging child, grown into a plain and pious spinster, full of good works'? Did you think 'thwarted'?"

Ryder's answer is: "Yes, I did. But now I'm not so sure."

Near the end of his life, Thompson wrote a short "shape poem" entitled "On a Crucifix" that is startling in its simplicity.

See

Here at last

Is

Love.

Those who have known only a very partial and sketchy account of the life and work of Dunstan Thompson may think of him as "thwarted." But after learning more of the story and dwelling with the achievement of his best work, the reader may begin to perceive the golden string that runs through the narrative. Perhaps the reader may even come to believe that Thompson experienced—and gave voice to—the love for which he had waited so long.

POEMS (1943)

Water Music

Over the river, sleeping, sleep your nights
Of never my delights, of famous flights,
Not mine, outshining moonstone stars, displayed
Like summer sailors from black water drawn
To dance on malachite, to prance parade
Past queens last-quarter afternoons of dawn,
First sunset mornings, break-of-day midnights,
O as the snow swans end their Rhenish flights.

Over the river, sleeping, sleep your dreams,
Where heir apparent or presumptive seems
Already king to Nibelung, gold dwarf,
Mock maiden, and the jewel box knave at hearts,
Each standing on the beach, each on the wharf
To wave farewell to you, whose birdboat starts
Rising from submarine savannahed dreams,
O as the mermaid is the merman seems.

Over the river, sleeping, sleep your love,
Ice as the crystal moon, so soon the dice
Of death, announcing lunar empire here,
Fall like the songs of lorelei, like all
The bishop's towers, like flowers, like every tear,
While you, child of the mist, at last, must call
Green knight from water grave to dive for love,
O as my eyes are seven on your dice.

Memorare

Remember, at this moment, O somewhere
The plane falls through the indifferent air,
No longer flying the about to be dying
Pilot to any over-the-border disaster, but lying
Like the boyhood toy, by bad luck destroyed.
    The lost lads are gone
    God grace them

Remember how, even now, when the ship sinks,
The sailor, paler than a pearl, only thinks,
Diving through destiny to be invested with coral,
Of himself—saved from the sea caves where no laurel
Lives—and so gives up a gay ghost at land's end.
    The lost lads are gone
    God grace them

Remember, also, as the soldier in amber fires
Too late, his nerves, swerving on exploded tires,
Plunge through the past to exhaust their history
In the silent, never again to be violent mystery,
Which the womb worshiped more than the hero's tomb.
    The lost lads are gone
    God grace them

Remember—do not forget—the numbered, anonymous spy's
Suddenly surprised, not quite clever enough disguise,
And see him, neither gallant nor grim, obeying
The code, sans cipher, of the classroom saying:
O happy and hallowed to die for a flag.

The lost lads are gone
God grace them

Remember the enemy, always remembering you,
Whose heartbreaks heartbeat defeats, who too,
Shedding tears during prayers for the dead, discovers
Himself forever alone, the last of his lovers
Laid low for love, and, O at your mercy, murdered.
  The lost lads are gone
  God grace them

Hyd, Absolon, Thy Gilte Tresses Clere

Your eyes like islands lure the wanderer now
From salt-sea travels, water world of tears;
And welcome, O as hyacinthine spring
After a wintertime, your lips allow
Expense for roses on a lawn of spears
To show the soldier who is killer king.

What wisdom has the heart which worships God
Only by indirection, by grace of gold
And tiger hair, extravagant like sun
Light? How is praise made perfect when the nod
Of a halcyon head exalts my hand to hold,
Heraldic acolyte, this sword-shaped gun?

The question never finds an answer: boys
Who take to talking take to drink as well;
And I, rejected now by heroes, write
My name like mist around the secret convoys
Of those I love, whose dogwatch kept, still tell
Glass beads for one another through the night.

You too are one of them. You also mean
The figure from the frieze, the scarlet page
At stirrup, groundfall, mercy in between;
So I must martyr you, must disengage
My heart, that sad spectator, from a scene
Where war unwinds you like a clock—but my age,
O myrmidon of doom, shall see you seventeen.

This Loneliness for You Is Like the Wound

This loneliness for you is like the wound
That keeps the soldier patient in his bed,
Smiling to soothe the general on his round
Of visits to the somehow not yet dead;
Who, after he has pinned a cross above
The bullet-bearing heart, when told that this
Is one who held the hill, bends down to give
Folly a diffident embarrassed kiss.
But once that medaled moment passes, O,
Disaster, charging on the fever chart,
Wins the last battle, takes the heights, and he
Succumbs before his reinforcements start.
Yet now, when death is not a metaphor,
Who dares to say that love is like the war?

Tarquin

The red-haired robber in the ravished bed
Is doomsday driven, and averts his head,
Turning to spurn the spoiled subjected body,
That, lately lying altar for his ardor,
Uncandled, scandalizes him, afraid he
Has lost his lifetime in a moment's murder:
He is the sinner who is saint instead;
This dark night makes him wish that he were dead.

What daring could not do, the drinks have done:
The limbo lad communicated one
Last sacrament, and, fast as falling, heaven
No longer held a stranger to emotion,
Who like a star, unsexed, unshamed, unshriven,
Was hurled, a lost world, whirling past damnation:
Circled by chaos but by eros spun,
The devil burned much brighter than the sun.

This bellboy beauty, this flamingo groom,
Who left his nickname soul too little room
For blood on blades of grass, must now turn over,
Feel for the fatal flower, the hothouse sterile
Rose, raised in no god's praise, and, like death, never
Again enjoyed, must make his madness moral:
Washed by the inland waters of the womb,
The salt sheet is his shroud, the bed his tomb.

Villanelle I

For George Barker

The train is disappearing down the track
Bound for the border which the gunmen guard:
It is not likely that you will come back.

More easy to defend than to attack
Your verses show the errors you discard:
The train is disappearing down the track.

You are so young the genius that you lack
Is time which makes the diamond point so hard:
It is not likely that you will come back.

The clever critic and the charming claque
Are just the justice your high court disbarred:
The train is disappearing down the track.

Your comet light flashed bright when night was black
And showed how holy heaven could be starred:
It is not likely that you will come back.

These are the cinders from the engine stack
That float across the vacant railway yard:
The train is disappearing down the track.
It is not likely that you will come back.

Villanelle II

For John Gesner

The dark is danger though it dawns each day.
Disaster knows me as a mother does.
The sun will set no matter what I say.

This paradise, or pleasure park, is gay
At noontime only. Night destroys the rose.
The dark is danger though it dawns each day.

Sirens are silent; panpipes cannot play;
Their melodies are mute; their songs dumb-shows.
The sun will set no matter what I say.

The faun must leave the forest, go away
To summer countries where Narcissus grows.
The dark is danger though it dawns each day.

So spring presents the garden god. This May
His murder is more marked than men suppose.
The sun will set no matter what I say.

The boatman takes my penny for his pay.
Disaster knows me as a mother does.
The dark is danger though it dawns each day.
The sun will set no matter what I say.

The End in View

Not always to beware the outstretched hand,
The friendly word, the loving look. And never
Forever to discover the arctic strand,
The winter kingdom where the snowman excites
No season of summer, where the northern lights
Are only auroral to the iceberg's endeavor;
The place of frozen water, the cold land.

Somehow to understand each other. To see
That the mirror image is a piece of glass;
The bullet, meant for everyone but me,
I shoot myself; the elegy, a celebration
Of gladness, not sadness. Let the hero pass,
Facilis descensus, the avenue of tombs,
His pride death daunts, his pomp the dust dooms;
All columns fallen, the arch gone down. But we
Are not heroes so long as the heart is strong
To praise God's grace in the one beautiful face,
Whose gaze, gold against the sun, an exaltation
Of indifference is. So let us like angels trace
High heaven with stars to make a morning song,
And let us, O Loving, move the mountains from their base.

Jack of Hearts

Loving you more than myself, I offer only
The mirror broken, O at the first word spoken
By you: quicksilver argent through all marrow
Of skull and skeleton; Christ's crystal token,
Spun from the showcase—the one place where the lonely
Hero, passing the glass, reflecting his sorrow,
Looks for the devil, and is rarely mistaken:
Behold the jewel for any fool to borrow.

But I am no thief. For this my grief is formal,
A manner, so to speak, of giving pleasure
To you, who measure me, but not with metric
Standards, nor assay my worth by faith in normal
Laws of balance. You cause the keeper of the treasure
To diamond-cut the bloodstone from the rhetoric.

II

There was no bell. Nor telegram to tell
Me: "All is lost. Flee for your life." Nor call
Intoned by the telephone: "Be warned in time.
For there's no coming back, no second chance."
Nor fancy glance beckoning me aside to rhyme
"Beware" with "There." Nor hand that appalled the wall,
Writing, writing, writing: "There was no bell."

Time is, time was, time's yet to be. Love grants
The absolution of the dove to temporal crime,
Breaks the mirror, stops the clock, and in the fall
Brings back the spring to every wishing well.
So in that moment, moment of no time at all,
What zenith bell you rang, what crisis chime
Pitched high, O ever higher than my angel chants.

III

Exaggeration of sensation shows
The poet loves a person not a poem.
So you, my dangerous darling, my delight
And doom, are like the tomb tricks Merlin knows;
The foolish fever, holidaying schoolboys home;
And, O so once again, the plane in flight.

All poems are praise, all lust a kind of love.
But I celebrate the fate of those whose diffidence
Led them instead of passion; who were of
That passive nation featuring the future tense;
The what have we here, better the half a loaf;
All looking-glass lads who found their class a defense
Against not being a bastard; those always above
The in-want-of-a-word battle. For them I write you nonsense.

IV

Here where there is nothing to fear except life,
I find the knife in the wound, the blood-red blade
Arrayed against my so-called heart. And all the art
Of witchcraft, such as I laughed at once, is prayed
For now. How if those killer sisters, crazy to start
Operations of love, thrice be bitch, each be my wife.

My destiny is hastened, O not by a star but a war,
And somewhere, yes, already, I march out to disaster,
Not needing to guess the place by blessing a better
One for you. But what does it matter whom it is for,
So long as the fact is death. Meanwhile, and much faster,
While my hands drop from the clock, your airmail letter
Canonizes tomorrow, and, though yet to be written, means more
To me than poetry, means not the furies at the door.

Largo

For William Abrahams

Of those whom I have known, the few and fatal friends,
All were ambiguous, deceitful, not to trust:
But like attracts its like, no doubt; and mirrors must
Be faithful to the image that they see. Light bends
 Only the spectrum in the glass:
 Prime colors are the ones which pass
 The less distorted. Friendship ends
In hatred or in love, ambivalence of lust:
Either, like Hamlet, haunted, doting on the least
Reflection of remorse; or else, like Richard, lost
 In vanity. The frozen hands
 That hold the mirror make demands;
And flexing fingers clutch the vision in a vise.
Each one betrays himself: the ghostly glazer understands
 Why he must work in ice.

All friends are false but you are true: the paradox
Is perfect tense in present time, whose parallel
Extends to meeting point; where, more than friends, we fell
Together on the other side of love; where clocks
 And mirrors were reversed to show
 Ourselves as only we could know;
 Where all the doors had secret locks
With double keys; and where the sliding panel, well
Concealed, gave us our exit through the palace wall.
There we have come and gone: twin kings, who roam at will
 Behind the court, behind the backs
 Of consort queens, behind the racks

16

On which their favorites lie who told them what to do.
For every cupid with a garland round the throne still lacks
	The look I give to you.

The goddess who presided at our birth was first
Of those in fancy clothes fate made us hate to fight:
The Greeks with gifts, good looks, so clever, so polite,
Like lovers quick to charm, disarming, too well versed
	In violence to wear weapons while
	They take a city for a smile.
	By doomed ancestral voices cursed
To wander from the womb, their claws plucked out our sight,
Who nighttime thinking we are followed down the street
By blind men like ourselves, turn round again, and wait,
	Only to hear the steps go past
	Us standing lonely there, at last
Aware how we have failed; are now the Trojan fool
For all the arty Hellenistic tarts in plaster cast:
	The ones who always rule.

We are alone with every sailor lost at sea
Whose drowning is repeated day by day. The sound
Of bells from buoys mourning sunken ships rings round
Us, warning away the launch that journeys you and me
	On last Cytherean trips in spring.
	There the rocks are where sirens sing
	Like nightingales of death. But we,
Hearing excitements, music for the ear, have bound
Our voyage to find its ending where the sterile sand
Spends pearls and coral on a skull. The sailing wind
	Is with us now and then: blows high
	As halcyon clouds across the sky:

Falls fast to doldrums while the moon is also young,
Untided, half to harvest whole. See how our sirens die
    Before their song is sung.

What we have always wanted, never had, the ease,
The fame of athletes, such happy heroes at a game,
Beloved by every likely lad, is not the same
As what we have: these measured methods how to please
    An indolent and doubtful boy,
    Who plays at darts, breaks for a toy
    The sometime valued heart. Why seize
The moment in the garden, on the stair, to blame
Our nameless Eros for his daring? Too little time
Is left for love. When we come back, what welcome home
    Will he award our wounded eyes?
    What uniform be his disguise
In dreams, when sleeping sentries always march away
Once more to war? Now is our novelty: we may surprise
    The faun at end of day.

Make no mistake, my soldier. Listen: bugle calls
Revoke your leisure like a leave, invade your peace
With orders on the run, and, loud as bombs, police
Your life for death. The poet's blood-brick tower falls:
    Even his vanity is gone,
    Which leaves the loser all alone.
    Not private poems, but public brawls
Demand his drumbeat history, the pulse that must increase
Until his heart is ransomed from its jewel. Revise
Your verse. Consider what king's killer did to those
    Who wrote their way between the shells
    That last delusive time. Farewells
Are folly to our serpent queen. She will not sign
Discharge of conscience for a masterpiece, but, hissing, tells

18

Failure in every line.

We are the mountaineers who perish on the slopes
Of heaven high and perfect Himalayan peak:
Exhausted by the cold, we can no longer speak
To one another—only signal by the ropes.
    Those best before us have, alas,
    Plunged through a gentian-blue crevasse:
The snow-blind flaw. Their glacial hopes
Shine as a stream of desperate stars, icebound, and bleak,
That mock their nimbused glory from a frigid lake.
Where we stand now, they stood much farther: climbing like
    Legendary guides. But traps
    Were waiting for their last collapse:
Inviting visions from the moon world air—misplace
A step to follow, dance to death. They fell, so we, perhaps,
    May do as well with grace.

Now noble guests depart for good, wearing our loss
Like flowers. O Damon, decked with asphodel, who moves
Among the shadow dwellers. But he shall hear the hooves
Of unicorns at gallop, see them, coursing, toss
    Their fluted horns above the cool
    Unpoisoned waters in love's pool,
    And, kneeling, lay their heads across
A beatific virgin's breast. The day approves
His passage: sunlight on the secret river gives
Bright benediction to his boat. Elysian waves
    Bear him, the hero, far from us
    To join the gods. Illustrious!
No words may worship him. The laurel is not all
That withers at the roots, since we, lamenting him, are thus
    Autumnal for his fall.

Armed, say you? Armed, my lord. So, likewise, you and I,
Who with the butchered ghost must stalk the battlements,
Shall watch—cold-comfort guards—how lonely lie the tents
Where strangers sleep together just before they die.
    Look where their banners in the air
    Are half-staff hung. The cockcrow dare
    Of dawn is mourning in the sky.
Our thoughts like bayonets blood time. What precedents
Of passion shall we use to brave the coward? Once
Bombs are as roses, will he kiss the black-heart prince?
    Honor, more heavy than the sea,
    May overwhelm both you and me
To give no quarter choice at all: gay boys, whom war
Won janizary; youths, who flung away their shields. So we
    Are *mort à Singapore*.

Narcissus, doubled in the melting mirror, smiles
To see himself outfaced by tears, and, sorrowing, hands
His ace of love to harlequin of hearts, who stands
The distant edge of laughter. Time's joker still compiles
    Trick score of triumph, trumps the queen
    To play his knave of emeralds. Green
    Gamester reflects the water guiles
Of palming, reads the gambled cards, and then demands
Another pack to shuffle. But the glass partner bends
The fate five fingers round a saint's stigmata, wounds
    By dealing diamonds from his nails.
    No marveled metaphor avails
To vantage this beloved impersonator twin,
Whose coronet, crown crystal, qualifies a peer. My voice fails.
    In your name poems begin.

Orphic Song

Midnight is time enough to call
Eurydice to life. Alas
For poets then, when crystal all
Walls of glass bend, if Orpheus pass
Along the corridors of hell.

She tells her devil he is bright
Light of laughter; is outlaw
To only heaven's purblind sight;
Who might, love's hero, singsong more
Than angels out of Charon's boat.

But he, goat, peacock, pretty boy
Of bells and wishing wells, cannot
Be flattered. He, the satyr, annoy
Him as she may, will clock the dot
Of twelve, alive like moon by day.

Away from him, she sees her life
Ascending passageways of death,
Turn as a burnt-out flame, a knife
Interned to stop her yearning breath
For false spring, April showered by grief.

Half harlot, half Elysian queen,
Whose lover praises no one when
He looks too soon, unseen
Eurydice must mother men
Like sunset sons who see no sign.

LAMENT FOR THE SLEEPWALKER (1947)

Lament for the Sleepwalker

The lion is like him and the elusive leopard:
Nine lived, he ranges—killer cat—my heart.
Green is the hanging moss, and green the jungle
Creeper: green where the gold plantations part
Their bamboo branches for a murderer's head.
In green courts he eats meat from the green dead.

See, like a rajah, how he ravens fine food.
The long claws fork their lightning; diamond, his teeth,
Glitter of jewel jaws, dazzle—glaze their mirrors
Black blood and purple, stained points of glass. Beneath
Lascivious fur, his regal muscles flex,
Digesting fire, the marrow root of sex.

At bat-call sleeps: at serpent hour is waking,
My beautiful and butcher beast, once more
The prowler from the palms; and stalks, O hunter
Hidden in death's ambuscade, love going before
The daylight with a leveled spear. What time
He gives by lemon tree, he takes by lime.

Sprung from his high point, Tiglon, Prince of Asia,
His forepaw threads through scarlet sockets—blind
Since the great nails pitted sapphire: ice-tipped needles,
Magnetic to their lodestar, flashing, find
Out violet veins, whose midnight rivers race
To Golconda for their trysting place.

Where skullbone banners, no pity flags, are flying
Before the cruel and radium caves, he lairs

His treasure. There, while jackals scream, Lord Vulture,
Wing caged in crystal, sings his subtle airs
Of praise; recalls how orchid adder hissed
Above the crypt when lion and lover kissed.

Nightmare is livelong by a never-ending:
In the most mandrake forest, I walk, love lost,
Through panther grass towards no good morrow. Agave
Leaves like hundred years impale my ghost
On yesterdays of youth. At crossroad stands
The strangler with his four and frantic hands.

The Lay of the Battle of Tombland

"Whatever you want is yours,"
     Said the Man with the Lopside Head;
"Girls, diamonds, and motor cars,
     If you'll love me, love me in bed."

So he prayed, and the sirens sang
     Their wrongs, O sang to me
Lost in the blackout, "You're young
     But wait till you're old as we."

I stayed where I was, afraid
     To leave the Club Foot Man;
"Behind the mirror," he said, "we'll hide.
     The dead have a death-ray plan."

"Welcome! Welcome!" the searchlights wrote.
     "The End of the World is here."
They spelt their names and then went out,
     And the poor lay everywhere.

What could I cry but "Bombs Away,"
     When the Man who was Hunchback spoke.
"O live through this, and be my boy,"
     He laughed, and his true voice broke.

"God, be nimble," the dicers begged,
     "Christ, be quick;" but they rolled too short,
Their fears embraced, and the whirlers bragged
     "In our heartbreak arms is sport."

The Harelip Man knelt down to drink
    Blood from the sewers, swore
"You'll kiss me yet, and you'll thank
    Me later, later, after the war."

Through air of flares the statues ran
    Shrouded in silk. "Be warned,"
They wirelessed, "for marble men
    Are the friends you never mourned."

O bathed in fire my mobster stood,
    The Man with the Artificial Eyes,
"Falling in love with love," he said,
    "Is falling in love with lies."

This piteous city gave up the ghost
    In the toll of all her towers;
Parachute princes held me fast,
    "Rest," they ordered, "the rest is ours."

This Tall Horseman, My Young Man of Mars

This tall horseman, my young man of Mars,
Scatters the gold dust from his hair, and takes
Me to pieces like a gun. The myth forsakes
Him slowly. Almost mortal, he shows the scars
Where medals of honor, cut-steel stars,
Pin death above the heart. But bends, but breaks
In his hand, my love, whose wrecked machinery makes
Time, the inventor, weep through a world of wars.
Guilt like a rust enamels me. I breed
A poison not this murdering youth may dare
In one drop of blood to battle. No delight
Is possible. Only at parting do we need
Each other; together, we are not there
At all. Love, I farewell you out of sight.

Songs of the Soldier

To Harry Brown

I

Soldier, the coward's hero, where
  Is your cocksure courage now?
Death blows the boys to ribbons. They were
  Your friends. Their eyes like lapis glow

With stone-cold brilliants, eyes whose fire
  Burned to a cedar ash your heart.
Dead, their razzle-dazzle bodies, bare
  Foot in bedroom, pull apart

As things of string. That baited lure
  The flesh, quick and fantastic, thanks
God today; tomorrow, and your
  Tongue tied, dumb mouth of hell. The links

Of love snap. And happiness, once here
  And now, the blood embellished rose,
Declines. They will come home no more,
  Those sailors from the sea, nor those

Soldiers, like yourself, from a far
  Country. You were their wanderlust
Or place of rest. Lack-luster, are
  They as dear as dead? In the past

You waited, excited, watched the door;
  They wait for you forever, not

Caring how long. No new friends wear
      Away your image, nor can plot

You damage. They keep true faith, their
      Loyalty is endless. If a kiss
Woke you sometime, still living, swear
      Love to the dead. A war means this.

II

Death is a soldier and afraid
    Like you. If he could talk, he'd tell
The world how he was hurt. This sad
    Faced, grave eyed, beautiful as steel

Young man, his sex a star, has pride,
    That sharp, unshadowed, surgeon's light
By which heroes are turned inside
    Out, their flamboyant guts put straight

Or lopped off. His dripping wounds bleed
    Acid, salt water, rot the strands
Of cotton gauze and bandages. Blood,
    Blood, blood dapples all our hands

Who lounge through war like girls in bed.
    Camp followers, base bred darlings, hard
As our frozen hearts, we loot the dead
    Of their fear, their fearful tears. Word

Of mouth, that snake-pit, says we did
    Our duty. But the lurid gin
Palace, where lust and money collide
    By the bar, then couple in

The gas light, shuts out those who paid
    Not sweetly for our common wealth.
These are no fictions but friends made
    Mock of by heroics. The filth

Which washes them like unction should
    Be for us as well. Soldier, that youth,
A drab death, might have grown great, had
    He been you. To love him, tell the truth.

Prothalamium for the Black Prince

Midnight. The gaydog heart bays moon and murder.
Our loneliness is like an island's when
The mail boat leaves never to sail back again.

You brought us love letters and drinking parties.
As tall sailors with yellow hair, your eyes
Widened our lives beyond the seagulls' cries.

Or as young soldiers new come home are giddy,
You told us of foreign books, how the girls
In port cafés looked after your watercurls.

We were your knowing guide to island customs,
Showed you a temple where the priest is slain
By humming bees hived in his golden brain.

On long walks with us through the native quarter
You heard our music, watched the ritual dance
Of beggars, acrobats, and boys of chance.

You were the charming unofficial traveler,
Who praised our parks, our public gardens. Where
The veiled statues stood you knelt in private prayer.

We were enchanted. Surely, you might welcome
An audience with our pearl and coral king
Who words the songs that wanton dolphin sing.

You smiled, and failed us. No, you must be leaving
Now, at once. "Time," you said, "holds nothing here
For the last moment. Time is to disappear."

Goodbye, the poet's friend, gone far as legends.
You sleep on shore, white sand your bride, while we
Wake with the green and never loving sea.

Nor Mars His Sword

To Richard Hager

My life is legends of the yellow haired
Who coin their eyes with money from my hand
And, seeing through me their good looks endeared
To the rough boatman, go, laughing, to a far land.
Each burnished boy, his riches squandered, spends
My fortune to persuade me we are friends.

You were the first—but may not be the last
Contriver, O death-in-life long lover. Time
Which we failed at school; time when devotions past
Reason ransacked us—what moonlight for crime:
That time runs out. Now I oppose a bad age
With courage. And you in a wrecked square rage.

Tomorrow I may not give you. But today
My heart, as instance, for your faithful watch?
Why, you shall have it, if one word I say
Lights up the nightshade by a striking match.
You turned me once against myself, and for
Your welfare I can offer nothing more.

At moments such as this my failure takes
Wing like the swan, and, singing, flies through death,
Air of the sad daredevil. Tears, these snowflakes,
Mantle the ruined duchies underneath
My eyes. "God have mercy on us both," you said,
And looked in the mirror at the glassy dead.

Angel of anguish, suicidal saint,
Dear friend with a sunburst for a martyr's crown,
I am your passing enemy, a faint
Fellow, but the broken voice is still my own.
Pray, rest—the world is wide awake. In heaven,
I believe, even our deaths are forgiven.

The Prince, His Madness, He Raves at Mirrors

In his dressing room, after the play, surrounded
by lights and looking glasses, he is found alone.

      No one is here. I am my own best friend.
This room of roses waits for me with silence.
Now, two faced double, shadow in the wings,
Content. My ending, it was quickly done.
"Viva!" they shouted, so I died for love.
And their applause, which handed back my life,
Rattled like rifle shots that babbling voice,
Blond Artifex, the seaweed sailor: "Hell's bells,
He's cold as gold in bed." But I heard drummers
Cheer from the pit, and from her chair a lady,
All emeralds and decay, threw down a kiss.
I am famous, as though I dressed in dollars,
Or wore my heart for signet ring. This name
Lights avenues of pleasure all night long,
Where drink and sex, the expensive wastes of time,
Embrace like dancers. False face, my exciting
Impostor, smiles from posters, while the sad
Young millionaire, the girl more beautiful
Than any spangled motor car, and I,
Gloved gunman with spasmodic hands, play "Double
Or Nothing."
               O Babylon, tall city held
Between the arms of rivers, sea urchins rove.
Pirates of grief, their pockets rammed with pistols,
Follow the perfumed suicide. His hanging garden,
Where I have dined at midnight, lion in chain
Of charming ironies, now shoots on fire.

Over sheer floors of silk the waltzers aim
To kill. But their host at music, his deep prayer,
Hears death in three quarter time to mix
Poison impassioned by the fragile pearl.
Those rowdy resurrection boys lie down
On black box sheets, where dreams, their sleeping sickness,
Stain the shroud quick-silver. Diabolist,
Whose legionary muscles move like iron
Filings frenzied for a magnet touch, conjures
Their pardon, but those riotous lovers speak
From wounds whose hearts are hard. Disastered Christ,
Hung from a gilded cross, weeps for the city
And the world.
              I am chilled, as though a star
Of mobs and children came by traitor's gate
And climbed the water stair to break his neck
On the axe king's block, all in winter sunshine.
His brain in ice, his guts a melting jelly,
As barefoot fellow bound for high-heel gallows,
Peer of the Presence like a spaniel licks
Cracked lips to ease his vomit back; then stumbles
On the ladder going up to hell.
                 Concerning Death:
The thought of death concerns me like a crime,
A work of art: for both the guilt is equal.
Seeing the searchlights on the river dive
Through sewage for a drowned girl; seeing the hooks
Caught in her hair, where once fingers were caught,
Saving a boy from drowning in metaphor;
Still seeing the lewd police reporters laugh
When pikes prodded her languid body past
The warehouse wall, on which she wrote in lipstick,
"For Love," and left a letter to the papers;

But, seeing no lover, only a water rat
Nuzzling her breasts, and orange rind her jewels,
I see the crime, the work of art, but not
The agony in the public parks, the tenements
Where fire bells ring the sorrows of the poor.
I am cut off.
           The Robber Prince, the rival,
His face my final faithful looking glass,
His hand ungloved, the blue revolver lonely
As love between his fingers, smiles. Now here
Is the Ace with great red diamonds in his hand.
O Mother, My Heart, O Heart, My Mother, speak
For me, remembering my name. This is my instant.
Next I know nothing, or know myself, and am
Triumphant. One with a veiled face shall value me
Forever. My crimes may talk me down with silver
Tongues of fire, or this be said to save. What
Mercy?
      Justice.
               I am cold to the marrow
And my bones ache. This cramp might come from kneeling.
But prayers were twenty years ago. Wordsick,
The rabbled spirit, riot heart, suppressed,
I long for peace, for sleep: no dreams, no drugged
Awakenings, and no noontimes after death,
When ghost light whitens the body of this lust,
And guilt lies tangled in the sheets. But nightly
Now the nightmare marries me, and in her arms
I wrestle with the naked rider. Lover
He is not, nor am I, but both together
Subtend ambiguous altitudes, construct
Passion with geometric pleasures, prove,
Demonstrandum, all demonstrative, the flesh.

Imperial pretender, the skull of poetry, threatens:
"Champion, you are unhorsed: the castled king
In check, the queen uncrowned, the bishops routed,
And far-off pawns troubled by their own concerns.
Where is that winning gambit now? Defaulter,
These ivories, once your friends, your only chances,
Keep time in the discard. This is spendthrift, cutpurse
Love, a mug's game, not for good. The roaring boys
With movies on their minds, the kindly killers,
Look for you to join the gang. Consider."
                                        My damnations
Ride after me on motors. They ride fast,
Faster than I can make my get-away.
Friends! Friends! I have no friends. I have myself.
And sometimes, at nighttime, all alone, have God.
This make-believe is murder on the stage
Where I become myself.
                            Enough of silence.
My aspirin followers, my benzedrine
Well-wishers wait.
                        Now, somehow, I must speak to them.

Sonnets to My Father

In Memoriam Terry Brewster Thompson,
United States Navy, 1891–1945

I

Exhaust this penny bank, the lust that leaves
You flat on your back, and face, eyes open, death,
Which cracks across the ceiling. Love, a wreath
Of cabled roses for a funeral, deceives
No one. Your discoverer with gold laced sleeves
Did not live for his windfall. O find the myth
Of the sea in tears. The sailor mixes with
Parakeets, perfume girls, stevedores and thieves.
The brine is salt and washes clean. But you,
Can you cry? The anchored heart, cut loose, swings
Wild with the tide. No home port in any land.
Here at your left side lies a lover, too
Handsome to be anything but kind. He brings
Sleep. And there your father holds your hand.

II

No doubt this death was not the death he meant.
The voice of the seashell broke against his ear
Sounding the bell buoys' "Death is to be here"
And to the sea was where he always went.
Because he was a sailor, because he spent
Time on the water, fleeting from the shore,
Surely he reckoned that he sailed before
His death. And yet no warship ever sent
Signal by searchlight, flag, or steel glass. But
He died in a white room with his daughter's love.
How was that heart, which hoped for happiness
To grapple in the whale's gullet, the shark's gut,
Able to breast the surf, the surface of
Dying at home? His life lies under grass.

III

Sea Lord, the sun in shrouds, and England rides
Like a death ship through the fog. Morning my
Midnight, now alack a day you lie
Under the far earth at Arlington. Tides
Trouble for a time their oceans, and on all sides
Of the world tears are for a moment, and history
Rises and falls. But the sailor's true blue eye
Fathoms the poor wreck of life: the wave abides.
Ah, Captain, you died at peace, although a war
Broke your heart, as once before your son had.
The years like roses darken, die: so fade
The roses on your grave. How the dead are
Easily put by. How the incomparable dead
Are easily forgotten. How still the dead.

This Life, This Death

This life, this death, to be met with everywhere,
In the street, the bar, the bedroom, on this page,
Which the dangerous stranger, or my best friend
Who looking from his picture seems to implore
A little courage, may not always allege
Against me by the poet's trembling hand;
This life, this death, to be met with everywhere,
I know now to be my good hope and not despair.

The lonesome midnight, the more lonely dawn,
When the lost last chance stands gibbering, a poor
Wretched fake made from my untidy clothes
And shadows over the bed and the green moon
Light, false, or the pale sunlight, false, and the pure
Temptation, untinged by grace, for laurel wreathes;
The lonesome midnight, the more lonely dawn,
These times I need rejoice and never mourn.

Among the mocks, the mirrors, murder books,
Where youth is spent, the runner lost his race,
And age, a waning passion for the truth,
Sets up his half-way house beside the lakes
But far below the mountains, so no ice
Ever reflects a blood rose or a death;
Among the mocks, the mirrors, murder books,
I may raise up the angels from the crooks.

In dreams by day or night, in dreams, in dreams,
When the unlocked furies spring, and the heart
Gives up its ghost, and there is no way out

From the maze of tunnels, the hotel in flames,
The free falling elevator, or the court
Of hanging justice, and it is always too late;
In dreams by day or night, in dreams, in dreams,
I am never left alone and the fear only seems.

The one last terrible gesture forgives,
Whether the world watches or not, for the clock
Tells more than time to those who go from home;
So the absent friend for whom this poem grieves
Held at farewell my past of futures, and with
His hand made me the present of his name.
The one last terrible gesture forgives
This life, this death. And childlike the poet loves.

The Moment of the Rose

A god of love among the silent flowers,
Your looks play rival to the sunlight view.
Late afternoon, the fragile, delicate time
Of sadness almost sorrow, overpowers
The languid air, as though these roses drew
Their perfume down long avenues of lime.
I see forget-me-nots are less than blue
When to their color your deep eyes are true.

Dear visionary, gloss the awkward guest
Abashed by plants and trees and foliage things;
Reflect this moment when the rainbow gives
Images of triumph to the sky—the least
Lasting enchantment; for past, perfect springs
Regaled those youths who lost their loving lives,
Some among gardens, some by seaside swings,
Or in a mean street, or where the nettle stings.

The dazzling slain companion you in arms.
Guardians, the watchers by the water clock,
They gaze like mica from a wall of moss.
These champions muster at the clanged alarms,
The one-toned coffin bells that muted mock
The rose, the willow, and the golden grass.
Against dead friends you need not ever lock
Your door, or wish them good or evil luck.

Now marble broken, now the gilt gone off
The princely monuments, one noble tongue
Recites historic love, this land of blood,
The murderous kings, the ladies cruel enough

In lace and luxuries to bear a wrong
Made madrigal, and lords who understood
Their sentence by a sonnet—these belong
To terraces where flags suggest a song.

The end of love is that the heart is still
As the rose no wind distresses, still as light
On the unmoved grass, or as the humming bird
Poised the pure moment by an act of will.
Death may be like this, but here before night
Sends us to sleep murmuring a drowsy word
Of prayer, affection, or the idle flight
Of fancy, let us praise the rose and light.

Of gardens there is much to say, but now
I write as witness to an English one.
Between black clouds and white, between the hours
This island rides the misted ocean, how
Debonair appears the gallant shining sun.
Here I have found, as after thunder showers,
The friend my childhood promised me, when on
A desperate feast I met myself alone.

In summer when these blowsy roses break
The heart, and turn from pink to purple, deaths
Like butterflies exhaust their heavy scent,
And fluttering through vermilion mazes take
The time of day away, and take our breaths
Away as well. Then tragedies are spent
By gardeners on their ravelled funeral wreaths,
And wraithlike weather brings the almond moths.

But now the stars of heaven sail like ships
Above the trees, and round about your house
Ancestral ghosts are wandering, long come home
From wars and voyages. Now this garden sleeps
In shadow. Only the rustling field mice
And owls on vigil keep the hours. We dream
Of the rose and happiness, we dream until
The end of love is that the heart is still.

POEMS: 1950-1974 (1984)

Ovid on the Dacian Coast

Publius Ovidius Naso relegatus non exsul
                    The Decree of Banishment

Airs from the sea blown back,
        The salt wind dense with sedge,
In the surf the sea wrack,
        And rocks ground at the world's edge.

With shells, with bits of quartz,
        With flints, with fragment bones,
Castaway, by dolphin arts,
        He starts, translates the stones.

The marsh birds wheel and shriek
        Above him, as he takes
Word after word from their bleak
        Coast of love: his heart breaks.

In place of gold, he sets
        A banished life between
Driftwood, and out of fish nets
        Roofs his loss with sea green.

Thus lives unexiled, though
        Abandoned, stranded, scanned
By the Dog Star only, for so
        Based, his poems are his own land.

Youth

Only the old are grateful. Not the young,
Who snatch their present like wild birds that feed
In winter; thankless, bear it off. Among
Those avid mutes, sometimes the wounded cede
Some gratitude, for they are old too soon.
Not so the strong-winged ones, whose jewel-like eyes
Glitter with instant fame, perpetual noon;
Who lavish on themselves a lifetime's prize.
Yet see them now as what they are—in flight
From childhood, eager, frightened, soaring off
To lonely falls, travail with traps, and night
Ambuscades. Those cygnets, swanned by grief,
Will be so grateful, it will frighten you,
Remembering yourself as thankless too.

Introspection

My eye aches, and I
Am too tired not to care,
As the dust glitters by
In the reflective air.
      Poems unknown
      Are hard to bear.

My eye aches—the eye
Is a mirror where
Self-deceptions try
Vainly to disappear.
      Things I have done
      Are no longer sure.

My eye aches, but I
Must see through the tear,
Take trouble to spy
Out light from the glare.
      Youth has gone:
      But age is not here.

Statues

I wonder what the models thought
When, standing naked in the light,
They watched the sculptors draw them out
Of minor beauty, recreate
Them with a grace beyond their own.

Perhaps that youth, with head inclined
Towards infant Dionysus, leaned
Too far, and, straightening, swung around,
So that Praxiteles complained
Because he had not held the pose.

Then, with his purple chiton on,
He had to bear the sight of one
Who seemed himself, yet nobler, shown
In marble as he might have been
Had he but always chosen well.

While wandering back through Athens, did
He stop beside a fountain-head,
And, staring in the water, chide
Himself on what he saw, and, sad,
Resolve he would be godlike too?

Perhaps that other youth, who grinned
At Michelangelo's command:
"Be always David!" whistling shunned
Such nudity of life and stoned
His fellow youths in scarlet hose.

But afterwards? On seeing how
They cried around him: "Beato!"
Did he, perturbed in soul, renew
The songs that shepherd king let fly
At the Goliath of self-will?

How strange for him, when old, to look
There at himself in marble, take
The compliments, half smiling like
The king he had become, and mock
Himself lightly: "The stance is good."

Those models seem to me wise men,
Who, troubled by themselves in stone,
Discovered then their true design:
And so their lives, I think, outspan
Time by a beauty worked within.

That tall Praxitelean youth
Is, with his sculptor, safe beneath
The tree whose fruit is gold, and both
Are works of art, who found their worth
On leaving many-statued Greece.

And he, whose Greek yet Gothic grace
Confronts an age of ugliness,
Together with that master whose
Unworldly spirit made him prize
Himself, sing lauds in Paradise.

Letter from a Mandarin of the Sung Dynasty

The marble boats have capsized
On the Lake of Imperial Rectitude.
Examinations for the Celestial Service
Have been postponed.
In the Spice Market the scents are bitter.
The porcelain makers do not work in color.
Their wares are white,
Undecorated, more fragile.
I have heard of no poems.
The painted fans you ask about
Are not seen.
Children refuse to study the Sages.
Old men are laughed at in the Street of Abundance
While waiting for the rice ration,
Which is now two bowlfuls a week.
Lanterns have been blown down
On the heads of ambassadors.
"Tribute-bearing ambassadors," they are called;
But they have the look of merchants
And are dressed in a reprehensible style.
On the Western Border there are victories.
Banners are flown.
The fire-works are of appropriate brilliance.
But certain provinces are no longer named.
Generals come at night
To the Secretariat For Concord With Inferior Peoples,
Snow on their furs.
Afterwards the faces of high personages alter.
Palanquins are in readiness.
I have been told of secret shipments to the South
Of silk-scrolls.

In the Jade Palace there are likely to be changes.
But for how long, I wonder, must we live
Without poetry,
Without painting?
The bray of trumpets scatters the pigeons
From the garden, as I write.
Perhaps it is another victory.
You are fortunate, during this Era of Contentment,
To have a post in the South.

Portrait Busts

Hard men—you see their faces everywhere:
Across those desolate desks, or, masklike, at
Some rostrum: lines and furrows, marble eyes;
Old faces, seamed and pitted like the moon.
And these were children, graceful, debonair,
Who fed their rabbit, hugged a clinging cat;
Later were boys, with poems like kites, and wise
With a young wisdom, whistling a small tune.

All gone, with even memories twisted round
To show them now as always—artful, shrewd,
Quick at the means to do another down.
Lost, lost that innocence, and lost the sound
Of gaiety in voices cracked and crude
From lying. Gone. Lost. Instead that iron frown.

Inscription at Sunium

Sorrow comes to all.
None is safe.
Each at times must sail
Through the gulf of grief.
In the spring or fall
May your voyage be brief.

Rescue, when you can,
Ships gone aground—
Where another man
Sees the waves surround
Him with their marble stain
And the rocks abound.

Mariner, be swift,
Let signals fly.
And you will straightway lift
Your own heart high.
For each to each is given
As our ships are driven
Towards an eternal shore.

San Salvador

Friend of the friendless, and the One who cares
For every lonely, frightened, desperate man;
Kind Heart, attentive to the feeblest prayers,
Hastening to all who do the best they can;
Dear Host, sole owner of the house He built,
Who, coming unexpected to the door,
Knocks, and, if answered, breaks the chain of guilt,
And lets the soul go free to live once more;
Shepherd, who seeks His torn and filthy sheep,
Rejoicing when the longest lost is found;
Father, who sees the broken wastrel creep
Towards home, and, running, lifts him from the ground:
This is our God, entreating us to prove
His friends and live forever in His love.

Three Views of Assisi

Santa Maria degli Angeli

The forest in the church cannot be seen;
Nor weeds and brambles underneath the stone;
The voices of the larking friars tone
Down the insistence of the birds that they
Are here alone.
              And in the chapel, Saint
Francis kneels, while crowded prie-dieus make
Their murmurous way.
                  Only the souvenirs
Preserve this touching place untouched: in paint,
On paper, china, cardboard, silk, they take
Time enough for poverty and real salt tears.

Santa Chiara

The empty tomb is filled with paper money;
As though by charity she might be coaxed
Away from home, suddenly to come to life
Behind the plate glass window, where her boxed
Body attracts the perfume of so many
Prayers, and deliver all the poor from grief.

She does not stir; the money drifts like snow—
The poor providing for their other selves:
Far off, the voices of her daughters rise,
"He hath put down the mighty": time resolves
The gold and roses at her side;—but new
Splendors appear, as each poor woman prays.

San Francesco

Beneath the Giottos and the Cimabues,
Which fade like every other kind of fame,
Down in this cavern, where the candles gutter
In a wind from nowhere, they have found
Your priceless bones—now barred off in the same
Way as jewels. And here the fluent stutter.
And here the experts are abashed. The sound
Of praying rises like the thunder of
A battle driven desperate underground.

And that is all. No paintings to admire.
No pious tinsel-touches to deplore.
Only the banks of flowering candles—love
Squandering *centesimi* on fire
To ring your stark unyielding rock around.
Here poverty, superb, is something more
Than riches gone. You've had your way. The poor,
At home here, crowd your palace, then go, crowned
In your likeness, towards that paradise
The birds and fish still preach about, allure
The children to. There cats are kind to mice.
There you speak for us to *il gran Signor.*

In Memory of John Keats

I see you battling with a butcher boy
To save a cat from torture, and I see
You, dressed for travel, stop at Wordsworth's house
And leave a message by the mirror. Why
These and not some other scenes? The sea
Washes where it will. Idly, the wind blows.

And poetry, you know, is not the same
As prose. Your letters, living like a sketch
Made suddenly by an evening fire, tell more,
Perhaps, than does the deep-cut marble rhyme
Suspended where the frieze extends to match
Its infinite progression through the air.

Yet poems are wanted. All can give the news.
Your letters only would but charm away
Winchester some Sunday afternoon, old
Cold rooms removed, with you there, laughing, as
I took your thoughts about that gloomy gray
Disconsolate uncherished town as told.

You are majestic, priestlike, when you write
Your poems and they give back your image like
Gold clarified by fire. Again I see
You, David—by prophet, poet, saint—whose light
Leaps round you, dancing, as you, tiptoe, make
The giant of failure fall to poetry.

O most delightful of those called by God
To write their names in water to His glory,

How you have triumphed once your death had done
Its saving work and you might, holy, add
Laurel to laurel from your crowning history;
One further leaf, and with affection, John.

Cardinal Manning

Prince, whom the people praised, though not the great
Men, milling with their money-boxes through
The palaces of chance and keeping state
From slums that opened out their hearts to you—
Your glory blazed through London when you died:
In gold and scarlet, you, etherial, lay
Among the ragged ones, who were your pride,
As you were theirs, even more starved than they.
Your portrait shows you robed in God's own fire
Of love, a skeleton of charity,
Whose eyes, too brilliant for their time, inspire
One most unlike you momentarily
To share the sight you, hungry, could endure:
Christ crucified again in all His poor.

Magdalen

In the delightful cadence of her voice
The wickedness appeared a fragile thing;
But when she spoke, her eyes, like desert fire,
Threw off the darkness of an old waste place;
And if she raised a hand to touch her hair,
The gesture, once it was remembered, stung.
Her odd distracting beauty bore the weight
Of years of jewels and youth grown desolate.

Had any of her flashing friends remained
To question her, the answer, framed in smiles,
Could only have provoked a sullen tear:
Her childhood too had memories to be shunned:
Banal, the usual causeways to despair
Had led her on: she too was one who fails,
Another of the hated self-same kind
Who also weep and have an unquiet mind.

The world she knew was all the world could be—
Charming, deceitful, glazed with color, cold;
A treasure house disgorging broken beads.
Sometimes her looking-glass threw back a ray
Of night light, and she saw the seven heads
Behind her, each an angel from the wild
Lost land of ruin—evil, avid, smart;
Clever at doing over a child's heart.

In scented shops her taste for trifles soared:
"But have you nothing pleasanter than pearl?"
An air of riches made her misery
Seem for a moment not to have occurred.
For this was never happiness, the slow
Effacement of God's image in her soul.
She aged in spirit: wrinkled there, her grief
At being who she was dreaded relief.

V

High in the noonday sky,
  His arms thrown open wide,
Love is about to die,
  With a thief on either side.

One He has welcomed home,
  The other prefers to hate,
Like the Pharisees, who roam
  In packs and wait and wait.

The soldiers there below,
  Bored and ashamed and blind,
Rattle the dice and throw
  Their lives away like rind.

The mocking scholars toss
  Their beautiful white heads
Far off; but at the Cross
  Who reads?

His mother, calm in pain,
  Adoring, and John,
The youngest friend, remain:
  Fair weather friendships gone.

And one other. She,
  Whose sins have had their share
In blossoming that tree,
  Offers her sorrow there.

Those tears are now for Him,
    Not for herself; she weeps
Outside her life; eyes swim
    Up from their own deeps.

His gift of sacrifice
    Opens her rusted heart:
With Him she pays the price
    Of love, that suffering art.

And so triumphant grief
    Makes her the fourth to stay:
Two innocents, a thief
    And a whore, together pray.

The Halfway House

The saints with the lollipop eyes,
    In horsehair and camelskin clothes:
The Greeks with the gifts that surprise;
      The Romans right out of their baths;
        And also the slaves
        Of permanent waves;
Oh, the saints with the lollipop eyes
    Are getting us out with our lives.

The saints with the lollipop eyes,
    Who collar the lion for a lamb;
Who feast on a palm leaf, and rise
      Like the phoenix, when Memnon is dumb;
        The fleas in their hair
        Likewise at prayer;
Oh, the saints with the lollipop eyes,
    Are running ahead of us here.

The saints with the lollipop eyes,
    Painted and perfumed in Rome:
The spendthrifts, who blanched at the size
      Of their debts, and started for home;
        The bankers, no less
        Agog for success;
Oh, the saints with the lollipop eyes
    Are paying our way out of this.

The saints with the lollipop eyes,
    Rebuking the serpent with grace:
The lauded-right-up-to-the-skies,
    Whose haloes shine round like a place
      With brightness that whirls
      From their glittering curls:
Oh, the saints with the lollipop eyes
    Are longing to show us the road at an end
      And each one a friend;
Oh, the saints are exchanging our pebbles for pearls.

VI

Alpha

Continue, Stranger, on the way you came:
Ignore these bones, sad Corydon's, who fled
Farther and farther from the thought of blame:
Be like the mica, hard and bright; be dead.

Beta

Stop, Friend, and ask those two young men from Rome
Who learned to love, the best way to begin;
Escaping pleasure, here they fought with sin,
And in a sandstorm triumphed: now are home.

X

"Be kind, be kind, and you will be a saint,"
The holy old men all together speak,
And see the traveller here as Heaven-sent.

But is this kind of kindness permanent
In cells that echo, while the tame monks work:
"Be kind, be kind, and you will be a saint"?

How has the traveller plunged in classic print
Been welcomed by these Noahs to their ark?
They see the sinner here as Heaven-bent,

And wash and dry his feet, obedient
To Christ, whose words on Judgment Day will shock:
"It is so kind of you to be a saint."

By kindness, write the mystics, here is meant
The daily going up of self in smoke:
At wrong times is the traveller Heaven-sent.

The Fathers of the Desert, childlike, scant
Themselves to give the traveller nourishment:
"Be kind, be kind, and you will be a saint,
And be yourself, and be, like us, content."

XI

"Prayer," says the Abbot, "is the price of peace.
In time, the khamsins from the desert cease:
The grains of sand drop down together, pure
In imperfection, and like rocks endure.
As for water, we have our own wells here.

This ordered life is not for everyone.
Never, to their surprise, for those who run
Away from love. Does not his coffee taste
Bitter? Ah, but how bitter is the waste
Of effort if why we give does not last.

You see, we are not playroom monks. Our hearts
Are in this, or we go. If not, the starts
And stops tell all the others what we ought
To do, and they persuade us. Had you thought
We stayed because we liked the quiet at night?

No, but you wonder what it is we do.
Simply, we love, and that is always new.
At Mass each morning we behold the Man,
The God, who died for us. Our prayer times can
Not last long enough to thank Him in.

And after dark? We pray then for the world,
That those who sin may not be suddenly hurled
Into the self-sought fires of Hell, but may,
By God's grace, live to love another day,
As we have done, and so can happily die.

If you will look down from the window there,
Across that courtyard, through the open door,
Into Saint Moses's chapel, where he has
Been leaning on his staff, waiting since Mass,
See, there, an Ethiopian works for us.

That old black monk does nothing but re-read
Words on gazelle skin, dawn to dark. Indeed,
He knows just how the Gospel should be sung.
With joy. And he is happy here among
Sinners, and is grateful for everything.

But that is all we have to show for some
Sixteen hundred years of being dumb
Before the Accuser, when he screams abuse,
Or, slyly, mocks us for being of no use
To others, and extols some busy place.

I think I have told you enough, perhaps,
For you to see why, when all things collapse,
Either a world, as with our holy saints
Who first lived this way, or, the Devil's paints
Worn off, a house of toys, men raise their tents.

Here we are safe from luxury and ease:
Few seem to care a lot for our goat cheese.
Now we have nothing which can keep us back
From seeing God. He fills up what we lack
Until our lives are all love for His sake.

The air we breathe is wafted from the sea
That mirrors Heaven, where we long to be.

We are not holy yet. We only show
The way to travellers. Later you will know
Much better from others what you should do.

This is a cap like mine for you to wear,
White as the Pope's, made from our own goat's hair.
In other places it may still convey
Some of the happy things we wish to say.
And you will not forget us when you pray."

XVIII

Macarius, the blessed athlete, speaks:
"The days, you'll find, will scurry now
Like little desert mice
Away from you.

Live no longer with the Greeks,
Whose time is all they have to show,
Whose marbles still entice
Men to a deathly hue.

Be patient in a land of leeks,
Learn how to market what you grow,
And throw in with the price
A smile or two.

So you will leave the love of books
For Love, who lets me let you know
He waits in a disguise
To welcome you.

For He is there among the wrecks
Of life: the old and sick, the slow
Unlovely men, the prize
Neurotic crew.

Their wrinkles mask His golden looks;
He smiles behind their sulky no
Response: in each His eyes
Are on you too.

So give Him love for love, who takes
Such pains to find you ways to go
To Him, and sacrifice
Will make you new."

In Rain, in Loneliness, the Late Despair

In rain, in loneliness, the late despair
Of streets like patent leather, where the stop
Light befriends the cigarette-lighting whore,
Her eyes sheltering a whipped mongrel hope;
And buses take their cruel primeval shape,
Mastodons of death grinding through the glare,
Their swimming sockets green with want of sleep;
And the sad city lies cold and wet and poor:
Then I have knowledge, hell is here and now:
How the soul suffers in doorways, is torn
On the iron railings, finds no footing true:
And I am one come from the films to know
No happy end, but that the heart is worn
Out among whores and storefronts and the lack of you.

Hearsay

It is said
That when the Emperor Honorius
Was informed at Ravenna
That Rome
had been taken by the Goths,
He was much distressed
Supposing
That the messenger meant
His favorite hen
Whose name
Was "Rome,"
But was at once consoled
On being told
Of his mistake.

Before we mock
We should be sure
That, on misinterpreting similar news,
We would not forsake
Our own grief
With the same
Imperial relief.

Alms for Oblivion

The end is always what you least expect:
The saints are lying in the devil's arms:
The damned are good and bored, deceiving the elect.

Be kind to animals and found a sect
For human sacrifice on dairy farms:
The end is always what you least expect.

Don Juan in heaven is Don Juan abject:
There cherubim fly after him in swarms:
The damned are good and bored, deceiving the elect.

Visions in steam, the Roman baths, effect
Conversions startling hell like fire alarms:
The end is always what you least expect.

The pirates, plumed with plunder, have been wrecked
On tropic islands, where their kindness charms:
The damned are good and bored, deceiving the elect.

But God is Truth, Pure Being in Pure Act,
And peace is in His will and on His terms.
The damned are done with, not deceiving the elect.
The end is always what you most expect.

On a Blurb saying that a Poet had given Five Plays to the World

It's one thing to give;
Another, to get them to take.
The first two were good;
The rest, a mistake.

Persian Quatrains

If death means nothingness, then spring deceives,
And every tree is treacherous with leaves
Which lure us to suppose that life survives
Even the winter when the cold lark grieves.

You see that tomb Shah Yussuf raised among
Those roses which he wandered through when young;
You praise the marble hemisphere above:
This greater dome of blue—is it self-sprung?

Last night the nightingale, while passing, cried,
As might have done a swan before it died,
And in the hush that followed, beauty woke
The souls of poets who, asleep, denied.

As men may see a thousand hopes go by,
Mirages melting in the desert sky,
Yet reach the real oasis of the palms,
So slave and sultan, each believing, die.

"Wine! Wine!" you say, and wine is good to drink,
But not, it seems, if you intend to think;
A little less, and you, perhaps, might find
Some not so bitter way to use your ink.

But are you what you are made out to be—
A cynic with the gift of harmony?
Or has some other written in your name
Lines which distort your own serenity?

For who can see the red rose, hear a bird
Sing out at nightfall one impelling word,
Or taste the grapes decanted into wine,
And, if a poet, call the world absurd?

Philosophers may teach more nonsense than
Could be imagined by the wildest man,
Yet foolish as they are, they seek the light,
Which, in your wisdom, you insist is night.

Both you and I have known the desert, told
Stories about a treasure-house of gold
Beyond the silence of those waves of sand,
And yet how differently our poems unfold.

You see three princes riding from the East,
Drawn by the Sultan to his wedding feast;
You hear the music from the river fleet;
But you, anarchic, feel yourself decreased.

The polo mallets strike the ball awry,
Which rolls across the field to graze a fly,
"This game," you say, "has neither rule nor goal."
And as you speak the players score their try.

Disparate though we are, we both make sure
Of color to enrich each miniature:
Yours is a scene of desperate revellers; mine,
A sultan in disguise who feeds the poor.

The new moon, rising, silvers each blue dome,
And silvers all the drinkers, staggering home;

So poetry gives its beauty every way
And silvers falsehood in a well-wrought poem.

Thus you can triumph with your sceptic smile,
Who watch Euphrates flow away like Nile.
"Rivers of Paradise," you say, and laugh.
But the poor go off to Heaven all the while.

The potter throws the clay and sees it whirl;
The jeweller searches for a flawless pearl;
In other booths the merchants bargain, but
In ours the pipes of controversy skirl.

For here beneath this deep melodic flow
Of lulling music comes the undertow;
Two rival systems battle for the soul,
And which is chosen only the listeners know.

You throw the dice, it seems, at random, yet
Strangely these numbers have discretely met
Before: the hidden sides, you say, are blank,
But now I show them, and you lose your bet.

Marked cards or loaded dice may here beguile,
Though at the cost of an hysteric smile:
This game is played for good: that drum, that drum,
That distant drum sounds nearer mile by mile.

Death, the last vizier, will inspect your heart.
Will there be nothing there but ruined art?
Only the saints are poets in Paradise.
"Too late," you say. But not too late to start.

No doubt the owl is hooting in the halls
Where princes walked; no doubt the jasmine falls
In golden torrents where no peacock stalks:
Both prince and peacock flew above your walls.

And now are elsewhere—prince, judged justly on
His minor judgments from his minor throne:
And peacock, innocent, unjudged, at ease
In gardens where no ruffling wind is known.

Why must you limit what you see to night?
Others expect, and not in vain, the light
Of dawn to dazzle on their waking eyes.
Poor poet blundering from too little sight.

Look, dawn approaches, silent and serene,
Foretelling what two poets might have been.
But now the sun gilds with a Persian grace
Both poets in a Paradisal scene.

Here let us end this disputation, take
Our pleasure on the blue ethereal lake
Whose waters show us Persia far below,
For at this moment now, you see, we wake.

Emperors of the Julio-Claudian Line

Tiberius

Was he as vile as Tacitus makes out?
A lingering legend has him ask about
Christ, be baptized. Was this how God replied
To one whose servant had Him crucified?

Caligula

They say, of course, that he had lost his mind
And could not be expected to be kind:
Yet hatefulness like his can still be had
In minor measure from the merely bad.

Claudius

Historian, whose histories are lost;
Imperial coin, which gambling soldiers tossed;
"A fool," Augustus called him; yet he won
Britain, which wise Augustus had not done.

Nero

Much given to the arts, he, singing, tried
Even the patience of the terrified:
When he was killed, the whole world held its breath
For fear that he was only acting death.

Stanza

They veil the palace tapestries at night:
Moonlight, they say, will fade a battle scene.
So time diminishes the bitterness
Of being young—those fear-fought days remain,
But with their savagery foregone. Success
Must be to have no memories to regret,
As greatness in a king, his peaceful reign.
Contentment, though, may still be had with less.
If tapestries can lose their wars, then let
The moonlight in, and from the past fade out the pain.

A Soldier in England

After the hatred he began to love.
After his loneliness he talked to friends.
Instead of deadly sunlight, here the rain
Softened a landscape to his liking. Of
The Army he could say: "Even a war ends,"
And feel close to his remote country again.

Was this not childhood recaptured? The books
Had told him how the kings wore crowns to sea.
The castle soared beside him now, and the swan
Embellished the river by his proud good looks.
The white rose, the red rose, these made history,
As might today the fair-haired Norfolk airman.

Slowly, not all at once, he could forget
The barracks where the boy, next bed to his,
Had cried each night, and he had been too afraid
To comfort, where that private, sobbing, let
His heart out to the pillow, no wife to kiss,
While other soldiers counted cadences or prayed.

Brought down to sham Alaskan mining-camps,
Solaced by Shakespeare's *Sonnets*, magazines,
He had learned much of life, and most was bad:
The depth of foul talk, garbage, tear-stained stamps
On letters scrawled by desperate bravos; scenes
From Dante—circle of the young and sad.

For some the test grew greater, and the war
Took them away, whose letter-writing ceased;

They had been shipped on death's pacific seas.
But he had sailed with lesser winds, and, far
From Texas and the desert trials, released
His heart, and now, in England, stood at ease.

Passage

The thistles, rooted out, throng in again;
The single regal rose is mobbed by weeds;
The plums, the pears, the ripening apples, rain
In the sun; and past summer plants new seeds.

The chaffinch looks around the world, and takes
His time with August: even wasps relax—
Late afternoon, their metric buzzing breaks
Off, as though they were bees and the light wax.

Here, or there, these common yearly things
Repeat, repeat, and gardens do not range:
Yet thistles, roses, fruit trees, birds, and stings
Come to an end, and the church bells sound a change.

These many soft declensions of the day,
So hard to take to heart, bear life away.

The Death of Hart Crane

Who said "Hail Mary" at the poem's beginning
Spoke as the angel spoke
To God's own Mother
Could you suppose
As the waters rose
Over a life of the saddest sins
She might refuse
To help you?

"*Mater dei*
Et mater mei"—
Come, let us with the mariners invoke
"*Mater divinae gratiae*
Star of the sea
Santa Maria
Pray for me"

How many times
Has she been summoned by those trusting rhymes?
Did they echo from the porthole
Just above the spray
Where the native sailors sang
At moments through the day
Of their mother
God's own Mother
Christ their brother?
Did the crying sea-gulls seem to pray
When the ship's bells rang
A clamorous *Angelus*
Mingled with the *De Profundis* too?

And all the bells were ringing to bring help to you

And failed
And the ship sailed
On into the translucent blue
And you were sinking
Under the green marble mountains
In the bitter sea

And did you think
She would forget you in your loss?—

Mary, who took you to her heart
With Tom, Dick, and Harry
All the sad sons especially
Whom Christ gave her from the start
When he looked from the Cross
At the bars and the bedrooms
And the Devil in the street
When He watched you through the Blood
That poured across His eyes

The bells
The bells had rung in Heaven

There on the absolutely even
Suddenly silent ocean
She stood
And the sea-roses clustered at her feet

"*Madonna*," Satan said, ascending from the water vaults
"This man has debts to pay
Payable on demand
Which are due and unforgiven
When one of our depositors defaults

We are left with no alternative but to pray
The Court, of which, *Madonna*, you are Queen,
The Court of Final Instance to decree
Judgment
Since it is passing pleasure which we lend
This debtor's payment has been long in great arrears
Here is the mortgage—death-gage—he was quick to sign
A little splotched with tears
Enclosed is list of mortal sins as shown
And there is interest at the usual fixed per cent"

"Demand?"
Replied your advocate
"You will demand
Nothing from this friend of mine"

"*Madonna*," Satan said in terror
"Surely, there must be some error
He is not—how can I best express negation?—
In the right state for Heaven"

La Virgo de la Mare spoke
"There is a place of preparation
Where love burns only to be joined with Love
And while it burns, the self-love sifts away
And so the soul takes on the beauty it is given

You know this
Do not, then, deceive"

The dolorous spirit seemed to sigh
As though with grief

"Of course—but that does not apply
He deserves the just desert he chose

He has, *Madonna*, brought himself to die
Despair has made him make
The profound mistake
We had the honor to suggest
Earlier in the bar
And we must now foreclose"

"But is he dead?"
Asked the Queen of Poets
Regina poetarum
As the twelve stars shone above her head

"*Si, Madonna, si*"
Said Satan eagerly

"That is not true"
Said the Queen of Angels
And placed her mantle twice around you
"He called this 'ageless'"
Saying so, she gestured to the blue
Empyrean hue
That colored all the sea
Which had become her mantle too

"He is still living—
Free to choose
Friend or enemy
He need not lose
His little toe to you"

And she who once had leaned above the manger, giving
Her love to God become a child warmed by the breath of beasts
Leaned over your poor wasted body
Which was supported by the silent subject sea

"Dear Son," she said
And held you in a mother's calm embrace
But though she looked at you she gazed
Into another Face
And saw the eyes alight like hers with love
"Dear Son," she said, and Satan seemed to weep
Over his own reflection in the deep
Impassive sea
"Dear Son,"—and in the silence raised
To a pitch of music, she besought
Christ for your soul

And you were saved

Since has she ever asked in vain
For the worn-out sinner caught
In his own toils
Who once held out a handful of small flowers
In imagination as she passed before him
Followed by her virginal angelic train?

So in your mind
Among the broken towers
Of pride
In the moment before you died
Mater divinae gratiae
She placed her Christmas Child
And you, awaking from what seemed a sleep
Saw Him as you had known Him
Meek and mild
When you were playing at your mother's feet
In the happiness of long ago
And all at once you chose Him
Utterly and forever

And your sins washed away
And the Devil went away
And you were at peace
Forever

Something like this, I think, took place
When you were dying in the sea
And brought an everlasting rest
To you, who in these recent empty livelong days
Simply self-taught, knew how to praise
God and the Blessed Virgin best

Now, with Columbus, you have reached
That shore where every care is beached
So, of your goodness, pray for me

Poem

Eros, his plumes bedraggled by the snow,
Came on me walking through the frozen park.
"Well met," he said, "the day is dying now,
So we shall talk together in the dark."

But there was light enough to see his face,
Those eyes of ice, that mouth impassioned stone,
The whole expressionless, as though a place
Where happiness and suffering were not known.

Early Poems

These are the ruins of a desperate day.
Among cold jagged stones
The serpents used to sway;
But now their empty skins, dull diamond tones,
Litter the lifeless towers.
The secret grief-enveloped complex rooms
A moment gleam with truth;
For, while the spinning spider winds
His way among the poisoned blooms
That loiter through the arches,
The dank deceitful foliage still reminds
The curious traveller: "Here is sadness
And the waste of youth."

Thrush as Minor Poet

A short flight.
A small song.
They give delight.
What is wrong
With being what you are—
Bird, not star?
A short flight.
A small song.

Fragment for Christmas

Dear Lord, and only ever faithful friend,
For love of us rejected, tortured, torn—
And we were there; who on the third day rose
Again, and still looks after us; descend
Into each wrecked unstable house; be born
In us, a Child among Your former foes.

On a Crucifix

See
Here at last
Is
Love.

Dedication

Your friend? I am. In every way I can
Be—failing often, yet succeeding too.
Not as an angel, simply as a man,
I make a present of myself to you.
What do you get? The shyness from my youth.
Also the gaiety bestowed at birth.
Devotion to you and, as keen, to truth,
My only value as God gives me worth.
Would there were more, much more, to make me shine
Now as in Heaven I hope to do. But still
You have my poems, and they are yours, though mine.
There is my meaning. There my gift and skill
Together worked the best that I could do.
And all, most gratefully, is given to you.

Afterword

Two Poets Named Dunstan Thompson

DANA GIOIA

I.

To sing is the work of a lover.

—ST. AUGUSTINE

Like most poets, Dunstan Thompson has been neglected. His early work has been out of print for seventy years. His later work appeared only in a posthumous edition that was never commercially distributed. No current anthologies reprint his poems. His critical prose has never been collected. His novel and travel book have become items for antiquarian booksellers. Although Thompson enjoyed considerable fame in the 1940s, his reputation evaporated within his own lifetime. Until D.A. Powell and Kevin Prufer compiled their tribute volume, *Dunstan Thompson: On the Life and Work of a Lost American Master* (2010), one might have said that the author had been entirely forgotten. Even now most poetry readers will not recognize his name.

Thompson, however, is a neglected poet with a difference. Despite his obscurity, he has managed to generate controversy.

107

Invisible in the broader culture, he has attracted a fitful audience, though few—both enthusiastic and openly partisan. In the forty years since his death in 1975, Thompson's work has continued to be read and discussed among poetic coteries in both England and America, though their commentary has rarely appeared in print. The people who care about his legacy have known it is good enough to argue about.

Two contradictory views of Thompson and his poetry have emerged, which seem to reflect an irreconcilable dichotomy inherent in both his life and work. Each faction has made exclusive claim to his legacy. For one group, Thompson stands as a pioneering poet of gay experience and sensibility. He was one of the first poets—and certainly the best of the World War II era—to write openly about homosexual experience. Although his language remained slightly coded—even straight sex could not be depicted literally at that time without censorship or prosecution—there was little ambiguity about the hidden world of casual sexual encounters he describes so powerfully in his neo-romantic and rhapsodic poems. An heir to Walt Whitman and Hart Crane, Thompson stands, to quote Jim Elledge, as "a kindred soul" to contemporary gay poets.

To the second group, Thompson ranks as one of the important English-language Catholic poets of the twentieth century. A neo-classical writer of cosmopolitan sensibility, he cultivated an austere and formal style to explore themes of history, culture, and religion. In ways that seem more European than American, the mature Thompson also used the long perspectives of Christian and Classical history to understand the modern world after the devastations, dislocations, and atrocities of a troubled century.

There is no question that Thompson's poetry falls into two parts—the early work published during the 1940s and the later work gathered posthumously in 1984. (There is no discernible middle period since Thompson published mainly prose in the decade after the war.) Each period presents a very different sense of the author—two divergent voices and concerns. Each period also employs a radically different style. The early verse is expansive, ornate, dramatic, and confessional. The later poetry is austere, urbane, controlled, and quietly confident. One cannot confuse the two styles, but is style the full measure of the man? Are there really two different Dunstan Thompsons? Does the youthful romantic really have so little in common with the mature classicist? Does admiring the poetry of one period prevent an appreciation of the other?

The controversy over Thompson's legacy has been further exaggerated by the fact that many commentators have read only part of the author's work and know only fragments of his life. Such ignorance is hardly surprising given the difficulty and expense of obtaining Thompson's books and the lack of reliable information about his life. There are no collected poems, no published letters, and no biography. The author himself complicated the situation because he so strongly preferred his later work that he declined to have his early poems reprinted—"a waste of youth," he called them. His literary executor and surviving partner Philip Trower has respected that request until now. This long overdue publication of Thompson's *Selected Poems,* edited by Gregory Wolfe, finally provides the opportunity to see this fascinating author's poetry in perspective.

II.

Beauty grows in you to the extent that love grows.
—ST. AUGUSTINE

The young Thompson was a poet of evident power and individuality. His stylistic signature is so strong that one immediately recognizes his work, even in short quotations. The adjective habitually used to characterize his early verse is "baroque"—an evocative but inexact literary term, at least in English. In Romance language poetry, the baroque style emphasizes mood and rhetorical display over narrative description; it abounds in metaphorical conceits, complex puns, elaborate syntax, and unusual similes. Thompson, however, has little in common with baroque masters such as Luis de Góngora or Giambattista Marino—except in his Catholicism and penchant for elevated style. Presumably, critics have imported the term to suggest the emotional and stylistic extravagance of the early poems. Rather than the rhetorical and metaphorical bravado of a Góngora, in Thompson's case the term evokes the high drama of baroque painting and sculpture—replete with the martyred saints, yearning nudes, and shadowy revelers.

Significantly, the term "baroque" also carries a pejorative sense in English. Not surprisingly, it was first employed to censure Thompson in one of the earliest reviews of his debut volume, *Poems* (1943). Howard Moss, later the poetry editor of the *New Yorker*, criticized the book's "baroque dishonesty," declaring that Thompson's poems "are moving, then, when they are most simple." Even when the poet's champions flourish the label approvingly, the term suggests that there is something at least potentially excessive and histrionic under discussion—a style that is richly fragrant but overly perfumed. The term will surely linger in Thompson's case and thereby continue to obscure the real source of the author's early style, the British New Romanticism of the 1940s. The precedent would have been obvious to the poet's early readers, but today it requires a scholarly gloss.

Despite his strong personality, the young Thompson wrote—with distinction and some originality—in a period style. Although one sees the American influences of Hart Crane and T.S. Eliot, his main influences were British—Gerard Manley Hopkins, Wilfred Owen, W.H. Auden, and Dylan Thomas. Thompson's key model, however, was George Barker, a leader of the neo-romantic revival. Now an author almost as obscure as Thompson, Barker, who was only five years older, already loomed as a major figure in the years just before World War II. A guilt-ridden, working-class ex-Catholic, Barker published his first book at twenty and became the youngest poet in W.B. Yeats's *Oxford Book of Modern Verse* (1936). His florid and fluent rhapsodies, rife with religious imagery and erotic reverie, proved immediately popular. With unintended prescience, Edwin Muir called him "a poet of genius at a still unformed stage." The tragedy of Barker's career was that his undeniably great talents never achieved meaningful formation. His work remained perpetually promising but persistently inchoate.

Most young poets borrow a style; few improve it. Thompson's accomplishment was to appropriate the elements of Barker's verse—the densely figurative language, pitched spiritual struggles, religious imagery, tortured eroticism, and self-dramatizing tone—and then employ them more powerfully than his master. Thompson takes the New Romantic style and pushes both the language and emotions further than Barker. In theory, this intensification of an already heated aesthetic would seem a dangerous strategy. In Thompson's idiosyncratic practice, it worked. Thompson created a poetic vehicle strong enough to carry his heavy anxieties—sexual, religious, political, and poetic. Here is the final stanza of the feverish and compelling "Tarquin," a portrait of a seductive sexual predator:

> This bellboy beauty, this flamingo groom,
> Who left his nickname soul too little room
> For blood on blades of grass, must now turn over,
> Feel for the fatal flower, the hothouse sterile
> Rose, raised in no god's praise, and, like death, never
> Again enjoyed, must make his madness moral:
> Washed by the inland waters of the womb,
> The salt sheet is his shroud, the bed his tomb.

It is always difficult and sometimes fatal to measure the sincerity of a literary work. "All bad poetry," remarked Oscar Wilde, "springs from genuine feeling." Sincerity is no guarantee of artistic success, but at the heart of most literature is the urge to make the reader feel the reality of the writer's experience. In Thompson's case, the question of sincerity seems unavoidable. There are serious criticisms to be made of his early work—especially its prolixity, emotional self-absorption, and circumlocutionary structure. Why do these overwritten and overheated lines nonetheless deliver such an emotional impact? What redeems the poem is its tangible sense of authenticity—*this is how it must actually feel.* This sincerity, in turn, seems to emerge from the confessional nature of the work.

The central impulse of Thompson's early poetry is lyric confession. The language is gorgeously decorated, the meter seductively steady, and the sins elaborately coded, but the confessional nature of the work is never ambiguous. The speaker compulsively bares his suffering and confusion to the reader—his hunger for male love, sexual guilt, painful romantic rejection, fear of death. Today these may be standard topics in undergraduate writing workshops, but in the wartime years these were not easy confessions to make, especially for an American in uniform. Thompson's self-exposure came at the risk of public shame and potential persecution—particularly the admission of homosexual affairs with fellow servicemen, which not only broke the law but also violated strict social codes of silence. "No tears in the writer," Robert Frost claimed, "no tears in the reader." Keening its vast and insistent threnody, the best of Thompson's tear-soaked early work transcends its own sentimentality mostly by its sheer frenetic persistence. All of the wrong notes seem small in comparison to its large, symphonic sweep.

The style of Thompson's early poetry is highly musical, metrically formal, and self-dramatizing. The language is packed with alliteration, internal rhyme, and assonance. The lines unfold sonorously in regular stanzas often mixing full and slant rhymes. There is lyrical repetition of lines and phrases. (The refrain is one of Thompson's signature devices.) The meter is almost always iambic, usually pentameter, a natural choice for a formal poet striving for resonant music. Thompson also occasionally employs iambic hexameter, which echoes the alexandrines of Charles Baudelaire and the Symbolists. Some poets underplay the metrical beat; Thompson accentuates it. One can recognize Thompson's hammered and alliterative style even in a single line:

> The red-haired robber in the ravished bed
> ("Tarquin")

> The head is human but the eyes are glass
> ("The Point of No Return")

> Narcissus, doubled in the melting mirror, smiles
> ("Largo")

> Where is the clock to tell my time of tears
> ("Where Is the Clock to Tell My Time of Tears")

> The strangler with his four and frantic hands
> ("Lament for the Sleepwalker")

Thompson reveled in the hypnotic quality of formal rhythms. His mode is essentially rhapsodic—an attempt to cast an emotional spell over the listener. The structures of meaning are not logical or expository but musical. His poems move in circles with repeating words, lines, or refrains. His phrasing is often stylized and artificial, remote from the colloquial. Here is just half of the ornate and periphrastic opening sentence of "The Point of No Return":

> See him now, how unhurried he destroys
> The tick-tock meaning of the nursery boy's
> Nostalgia for love's never-never land,
> And, fairy-story prince turned toad, spews out...

Thompson's densely crafted poems communicate mostly through inference and association. (Here one sees the influence of Hart Crane, the master of lyric indirection.) Thompson's aesthetic is auditory; the poems are meant to be heard. The rhetoric is overtly dramatic—usually spoken by an "I" often addressing a mysterious "you." "Water Music," which opens Thompson's first volume, *Poems*, begins:

Over the river, sleeping, sleep your nights
Of never my delights, of famous flights,
Not mine, outshining moonstone stars, displayed
Like summer sailors from black water drawn
To dance on malachite, to prance parade
Past queens last-quarter afternoons of dawn,
First sunset mornings, break-of-day midnights,
O as the snow swans end their Rhenish flights.

This passage is so flamboyantly overwritten that it acquires, amid its studied decadence, a sort of innocent and awkward charm. Ignoring the austerities of modern poetry, it unabashedly aspires towards the condition of music—the ripest late romantic music. Indeed, the author's intent is to *charm* in the older sense of creating an enchantment. Thompson casts a spell to bring the reader—and in a different way his lover—into a dark world that might otherwise seem forbidding. Seen from this perspective, Thompson's elaborate style is not simply a means to camouflage his homoerotic subject matter, it is also a musical formula to seduce the reader into feeling the private experiences being described.

"Water Music" presents its subject both directly (a nocturne sung to an absent lover) and indirectly (the images from the nocturnal world of rough trade along the docks). No degree in cryptography is required to decode the images of "summer sailors," "queens," and "swans." In Thompson's early books, the speaker is simultaneously intoxicated by the pleasures of casual sex and repelled by its predatory and reckless nature. No American poet had ever presented the homosexual milieu of the modern metropolis so frankly or so memorably. Auden had universalized the language of his love poems to mask their gay identity. Thompson's imagery is specifically homosexual. These are elegies on what Edward Field has called "pickups in the dark." Thompson's poems neither explicate nor document this underworld. Instead, they simply inhabit this secret city in vividly personal terms. In his combination of high romantic music, urban angst, and dark sexuality, the young Thompson found his distinctive voice.

III.

The punishment of every disordered mind is its own disorder.
—ST. AUGUSTINE

The obsessive theme of Thompson's early work is the doomed relationship between sex and love in a perilous world. Even when he deals with other subjects, notably war and death, they are viewed through an erotic lens. Passionate, impulsive, and melancholy, these are the poems of a vulnerable young man, not sure of his place in the world and afraid of a war he cannot escape. The speaker's voice is so strongly defined—in both the best and worst poems—that a unified, autobiographical persona emerges whose erotic ardor and existential panic permeate both of Thompson's early volumes. The sexual vision is dark and dangerous. "The boy who brought me beauty brought me death," the speaker laments in "Articles of War"—one of the many lines in Thompson's work that prefigure the poetry of the AIDS era. Sexual beauty is accompanied by deception and menace, "For the devil, good-looking as a movie star, / Moves among us." Lost in a carnal wilderness in a treacherous time, the speaker longs for the certainty of a true, defining love. This repeated dream of a perfect and enduring union will prove to be what links Thompson's early poetry to his later work.

Thompson is a war poet of odd originality. He depicts World War II not as a battlefield or training ground—the usual settings of his soldier-poet contemporaries—but presents it indirectly through an urban nightscape of young men seeking furtive pleasure as they powerlessly await their destinies. The war is lethally real, but it remains elsewhere and invisible. The young soldier's anxiety is one of Thompson's recurring themes, but it usually serves as background for the erotic dramas unfolding in the poems. War sometimes serves simultaneously as subject and metaphor, as in one of Thompson's most compressed and accomplished poems, "This Loneliness for You Is Like the Wound":

This loneliness for you is like the wound
That keeps the soldier patient in his bed,
Smiling to soothe the general on his round
Of visits to the somehow not yet dead;
Who, after he has pinned a cross above
The bullet-bearing heart, when told that this
Is one who held the hill, bends down to give
Folly a diffident embarrassed kiss.
But once that medaled moment passes, O,
Disaster, charging on the fever chart,
Wins the last battle, takes the heights, and he
Succumbs before his reinforcements start.
Yet now, when death is not a metaphor,
Who dares to say that love is like the war?

This sonnet unfolds as a single extended simile, a metaphysical conceit that might actually be called baroque in the spirit of Giambattista Marino: the lover's loneliness is like a soldier's wound. Through synecdoche, the speaker then becomes the heroic, dying soldier who bears the wound. Reveling in the pathos of the situation, the speaker oddly resists its heroic implication. He presents the heroism ironically as a "folly" in a grotesque death scene with the general kissing the doomed man. The sonnet teeters on the edge of sentimentality and self-pity, but before the reader can bring this charge to the poem, the speaker delivers his own stern verdict in the self-lacerating final couplet, which dismisses the poetic fiction he has so carefully constructed. (The powerful use of the Shakespearean sonnet's closing couplet recalls a slightly earlier Shakespearean sonnet of the period, which also uses the war as a metaphor for personal anxiety—"For My Daughter" by Weldon Kees, a poet Thompson published in *Vice Versa*.)

The characteristic virtues of Thompson's early style—its extravagant music, feverish tone, coded eroticism, and circular structure—become its weaknesses when overextended. Composing his poems in formal stanzas, Thompson often tries to sustain his volatile and emotive tunes like a singer who repeats a refrain one time too many. The early poems are unabashedly ambitious—extended lyric odes in the romantic (and New Romantic) manner. The grandest of these odes is "Largo," the central work in *Poems*. Cast in an elaborate fifteen-line rhymed stanza of Thompson's own design, "Largo" stretches across 180 lines—longer than Keats's three greatest odes combined. Full of powerful feeling and lyric invention, this impressive exercise in the sublime is so fraught with literary allusion and histrionic gesture that it cannot carry the weight of its own aspirations. *Poems* also contains two other long sequences, "Articles of War" and "Images of Disaster," each of which runs eight pages, but neither poem summons even the intermittent power of "Largo." Thompson is at his best when most concentrated. Perhaps his finest early poem, "Tarquin," the chilling portrait of a ravishing predator, runs only three eight-line stanzas (in an intricate double-envelope rhyme scheme). It is surely significant that so many of Thompson's best poems, early and late, are sonnets. Fervor requires a framework.

IV.

What am I to you that you command me to love you?

—ST. AUGUSTINE

Thompson returned to Catholicism in 1952. This decision, which reshaped his poetry, grew out of a new stability in his personal situation. The first half of his life had been largely itinerant; the second part settled securely in the village of Cley next the Sea in Norfolk. He had never before resided in the country. The quiet pace and solitude provided contemplative space that allowed him to reexamine his religious beliefs. Thompson's literary success had never been commercial, but he had enjoyed considerable recognition since his early twenties. As his public career faded after the failure of his novel, Cley also protected him from both the cultural competition and financial pressures of London. Norfolk's isolation allowed him to moderate the heavy social drinking that had characterized his New York and London years. His inner life calmed. His turbulent search for "the always loving heart" had led him to Trower, his spiritual hungers back to his childhood faith. "I'm so grateful to God for keeping me hidden away in this unknown village," he remarked shortly before his death. Not surprisingly, these profound changes transformed his poetry, though not exactly in the ways some critics have maintained.

A common assumption about Thompson's career is that he changed from a glorious gay pagan celebrating the world, the flesh, and the devil to a pious Catholic contemplating eternity, the soul, and salvation. Such a neat dichotomy makes it easy to generalize about the poetry. The problem is that a careful study of the work itself does not support the theory that Thompson changed (in Edward Field's pithy but inaccurate formula) "from brilliant bad boy to repentant sinner." The poems tell a more complicated and interesting story. They demonstrate both continuities and dislocations in his work. They also suggest that Thompson's main transformation was not theological but emotional.

There is no confusing Thompson's early and later verse. They not only differ in style; the tone, manner, and subjects of the two periods also bear little resemblance to one another. If Thompson's early verse is flamboyantly neo-romantic, the later work is calmly neo-classical. It eschews emotional fervor for measured reflection. No longer agonizingly searching for his place in the world, the poet speaks from the security of a meaningfully situated life. A reader may disagree with Thompson's choices—some proponents of the early work have—but there is no disputing the psychological and emotional stability that characterizes the later poems. "I owe my heart / Unfettered and my soul at rest. / To you, who offer more than all my art / Can match," he writes in a late poem to Trower. A critic may miss the youthful *Sturm und Drang*; Thompson did not. "Only the old are grateful," he writes, "not the young."

Freed from the traumatic struggles that had previously formed its central subject, Thompson's poetry either had to change or sink into self-parody. His solution was to reinvent himself—from a Dionysian romantic with a single lyric style and subject into an Apollonian classicist exploring a great variety of subjects, forms, and genres. His style cooled, becoming more austere and controlled. The tone shifted from vatic to conversational. The growth of his verse technique is also noteworthy. If Thompson's early work is characterized by its masterful use of iambic pentameter, the later poetry displays metrical diversity and formal experimentation. His prosodic patterns change from page to page. For the first time he uses free verse. No longer locked into a single rhapsodic mode, Thompson writes dramatic monologues, narratives, hymns, satires, epigrams, epistles, devotions, discursive meditations, as well as short lyrics. Thompson also became prolific. The "Red Book," as the posthumously published *Poems: 1950–1974* is often called, contains five times as many poems as the two early books combined. It is not surprising that readers smitten by the early poems find the later work foreign. It changed radically in most respects. What unites Thompson's earlier and later work is his personal identity as both gay and Catholic. The expression of that complicated double identity differs significantly, but it persists as an animating presence. The obvious fact that some of Thompson's gay advocates and Catholic admirers find the combination troublesome does not alter its continuity.

It is a great mistake to divide Thompson's career into Catholic and non-Catholic periods. Roman Catholicism haunts all of his writing, even the novel and travelogue. The early poetry is as deeply and explicitly theological as the later work. What mostly differs is the speaker's perceived relationship toward grace and redemption. Edward Field's formula is exactly backwards: only in Thompson's early work does the persona of the guilt-ridden sinner appear. This torturously divided soul, vacillating between carnal desire and spiritual despair, serves as the protagonist of the early work. If the young Thompson was indeed a "brilliant bad boy," he was also the very poster child of Catholic guilt. For him, sexual inebriation inevitably led to a theological hangover. By contrast, the calm and grateful persona of the later work is unconcerned with guilt or repentance.

The title of the early poem "Memorare," for instance, which means "remember" in Latin, alludes to a popular Catholic prayer of "guilty and sorrowful" supplication to the Virgin Mary. On a literal level, "Memorare" is a war poem in the form of a benediction for the "lost lads" killed in battle on earth, air, and sea. Oddly for an American poem written in the aftermath of the Battle of Britain and London Blitz, Thompson's lament mourns all the dead, allied or enemy, who share physical destruction, erotic desolation, and spiritual abandonment. Published a month before Pearl Harbor, the poem's neutrality was not yet politically problematic, but this verse prayer remains the strangest war poem of the period—simultaneously a religious lament and homoerotic elegy for the young male dead. The dead lads in uniform are so explicitly eroticized as lovers, often in homosexual terms—"a gay ghost at land's end," for instance—that it is difficult not to feel "Memorare" as a universal gay lament. It is unclear who the "you" addressed in the poem is—God, the Virgin Mary, all enlisted men, humanity itself, or just the poet—though its devotional rhetoric suggests a supernatural agency. Whomever it invokes, "Memorare" never ceases to be a prayer of both curtailed love and sorrowful supplication. It concludes:

Remember the enemy, always remembering you,
Whose heartbreaks heartbeat defeats, who too,
Shedding tears during prayers for the dead, discovers
Himself forever alone, the last of his lovers
Laid low for love, and, O at your mercy, murdered.
 The lost lads are gone
 God grace them

To miss the Catholicism in Thompson's early work is to misread it. Although the early lyrics deal obsessively with love and sex, the context in which the poet presents his erotic struggle is theological and specifically Catholic. Here is a stanza from one of Thompson's most explicitly sexual poems, "The Point of No Return," a nightmare vision of a gay Times Square hustler and drug addict:

What welter of the womb that air breath day
The serpent signified once more in clay:
Later, the data of a Christ-crossed class
The garbage gift of faith, slag heap of hope,
Concerning charity—the sounding brass:
Those cardinals triple crowned this antipope,
Whose keys are skeleton, whose ring is gay
With fools for jewels, whose blessings playboys pray.

In eight lines, one finds twelve Catholic images and allusions: the serpent, Christ, the cross, the three theological virtues of faith, hope, and charity, cardinals, the papal crown, the antipope, the keys and ring of St. Peter, and a phrase from St. Paul's First Epistle to the Corinthians. (One could press four further claims—womb, clay, blessings, and pray—but the point is already made.) Why is there such an extraordinary density of sacred imagery in a poem ostensibly about a street hustler? Thompson's feverish dramas exist in a theological framework. The sordid and sexual are inseparable from the supernatural.

121

There has been a hesitation among both gay and Christian readers to recognize that Thompson's homosexuality and Catholicism co-exist throughout his career. Just as the early poems are saturated with religion, the later work continues to reflect his gay identity—not perhaps in ways consistent with current orthodox opinion but nonetheless apparent. Sexuality has many expressions, including celibacy. Thompson's return to Catholic practice did not change his sexual orientation or eradicate his libido; it only provided the spiritual means to sublimate eros into agape. (Trower's unpublished memoir makes it clear that neither man denied his sexual orientation, however much they controlled its physical expression.) The "Red Book" contains several love poems to Trower, which may be chaste but are nonetheless full of passionate devotion to the man Thompson felt had redeemed his life.

There is also a common notion that Catholic poetry is a literature of saintly and well-behaved writers—a pious cliché shared by some Catholic and secular critics. This platitude has no basis in either theology or literary history. There is, of course, a great tradition of Catholic devotional literature from Boethius and Hildegard von Bingen to Thomas Merton and Simone Weil. Most Catholic imaginative literature, however, has been obsessed with sin. To be a Catholic is to recognize one's self as a sinner in a fallen world, and the central narrative of Catholic literature is the sinner's difficult journey toward salvation. Dante's *Commedia*, which begins in the dark wood of the author's own depravity, presents the full journey of the spirit from perdition to redemption. Many great writers, however, have portrayed only the darker part of the journey—often because that is where their own lives have stalled. Take, for instance, two authors whom Thompson greatly admired, François Villon and Charles Baudelaire. They were both self-proclaimed sinners, who declared they were likely destined for damnation. Baudelaire and Villon were no less Catholic for their sinfulness. Like salvation, damnation has its literary canon. Catholicism is a faith and worldview, not an outcome. From this perspective, Thompson's early poetry, which portrays his tormented struggle toward redemption, is both a landmark in American gay literature and his greatest contribution to modern Catholic literature.

Ironically, Catholicism is actually less visible in Thompson's later work. He does not disguise his faith, but he doesn't so habitually present it. *Poems: 1950-1974* contains some devotional poems, but religion is not its primary topic. The central subject is quite secular, namely history. The older Thompson obsessively ponders the past as a window into the human condition. His interests range from India and China to the United States and Panama, but his main focus is Europe, especially its ancient history. Thompson meditates on the lives of emperors, tyrants, philosophers, poets, and soldiers. He imagines "Ovid on the Dacian Coast," "Hannibal at the Armenian Court," and "Virgil at Brundisium." There are over a hundred historical poems in the posthumous collection. Thompson's subject matter is notably similar to that of another gay Christian poet fascinated by history, Constantine Cavafy, a lax and lubricious yet loyal Greek Orthodox. Thompson writes poems on historical Christian subjects, such as his epigrammatic sequence on St. Augustine and his passionate sonnet on Cardinal Manning, the great Victorian champion of social justice for the poor. But usually Thompson, like Cavafy, finds sinners more interesting than saints. Of course, there is a case to be made that Thompson's choice of history as his subject betrays his essentially Catholic imagination, which takes as its natural purview the long perspective from the present back to the time of Christ and the Caesars.

The mature Thompson also reveals a surprising gift for epigram, a linguistic compression impossible to predict from his expansive early work. The "Red Book" is full of epigrammatic verse, some self-contained, some remarkably built into sequences. Appropriating the classical tradition of Martial and *The Greek Anthology*, Thompson uses the form to ponder eminent figures of antiquity in superbly pointed epigrams on Seneca, Tacitus, Apollodorus of Athens, Caligula, Nero, and many others. In "Horace," Thompson neatly anatomizes the great Latin poet in a way that touches on the tensions and temptations of his own literary career:

> Perfection measured into every part;
> Nothing is wanting save, perhaps a heart;
> But when you are so clever from the start,
> Love almost always loses out to art.

V.

Take up and read.
—ST. AUGUSTINE

There is a final factor to consider in Thompson's later development. In middle age a writer gains perspective on his own life and work. He also better understands the careers of his contemporaries. Thompson's early adulthood was characterized by passionate excess. Both his poetry and literary identity emerged from that intense but precarious existence, an unstable mix of creativity and anxiety, love and promiscuity, exuberant sociability and alcoholism. As the fuel that fired his poetry, Thompson's life risked becoming aestheticized into a self-consuming artifact. Settled in Norfolk, he pondered the lethal toll that alcoholic disorder and emotional exhibitionism had taken on his contemporaries. "Some I knew / Took to drink / And died gladly," Thompson writes in "Memoirs," observing how many of his contemporaries were destroyed by sex or alcohol. "There were writers / Who did not write / Or wrote badly." Dylan Thomas had died at 39. George Barker had sunk into self-parody. (Hart Crane's alcoholic decline and early suicide haunted Thompson, eventually becoming the subject of one of his last, longest, and worst poems.) The failure of New Romanticism was not only aesthetic but moral; it fostered a voyeuristic cult of the self-destructive artist pushing experience to the limit for the delectation of the audience. A quarter century later the pathological tendency would reemerge as Confessional poetry and contribute to the deaths of John Berryman, Anne Sexton, and others. Thompson must have felt that he had pushed that style of both life and poetry far enough. To survive meant to change.

If critics have not yet done full justice to Thompson's early work, the later poetry remains mostly unstudied and unknown. Anyone evaluating it faces three major obstacles—its abundance, diversity, and varying quality. There are 259 poems in the posthumous volume, many of them long. By comparison there were only 45 poems in the two early collections. The late poems also divide into many different forms and genres, some of which seem more natural to Thompson's talents than others. All of Thompson's work is uneven. The second half of *Poems* (1943), for instance, is markedly inferior to the first half. *Poems: 1950-1974* is full of weak or minor poems. Thompson's penchant for travel poems, in particular, resulted in a kind of elegant verse journalism. The "Red Book" contains dozens of colorful but not especially memorable views of foreign cities and landscapes. The travel poems are perceptive and intelligent but lack emotional force and personal connection. Likewise some of the religious poetry is diffuse, prosaic, or sentimental. As in the early work, compression focuses Thompson's gifts; the best devotional poems are mostly short. But the "Red Book" also reveals poetic growth. The title of one of the best late poems, "Introspection," characterizes one particularly compelling change. Here the aging poet ponders his own romantic origins with empathy and insight: "My eye aches—the eye / Is a mirror where / Self-deceptions try / Vainly to disappear." In poems such as "Introspection," "Youth," "In Rain, in Loneliness, the Late Despair," thought is animated by powerful emotion. The two Dunstan Thompsons, for a moment at least, become one.

Dunstan Thompson is not a major poet, but he is also not a minor writer in the conventional sense of doing a few things exquisitely well. He is ambitious, original, mercurial, and uneven in equal measures. His central themes—love, sex, desire, faith, war, and history—are not minor subjects. When he fails, which is often, it is not from timidity but because he reaches for something beyond his capacity to convey. He wrote too much and often too obsessively about the same subjects. Reading him, one must overlook the flaws to find the virtues. Thompson did not change American poetry. He burned brightly for a few years, and then disappeared from public view. He left no direct literary heirs, but he has sustained a following for half a century. His voice remains vital and genuinely expressive. Thompson occupies a unique place in both Catholic and gay American letters, as well as in the literature of World War II. He will never be a popular poet, but there will be readers drawn to the passions he explores. "Deep calleth unto deep." They will not find his like elsewhere.

Endnotes

1. Dunstan Thompson, *Poems: 1950–1974* (Bungay, England: The Paradigm Press, 1984). Known to some as the "Red Book" (for the color of the dust jacket), this posthumous collection, edited by Philip Trower, is still available through St. Augustine's Press. For information, email bruce@staugustine.net. At 361 pages, the volume indicates just how much poetry Thompson wrote in the latter phase of his life.

2. Much of the biographical information we have about Dunstan Thompson comes from his longtime companion and literary executor, Philip Trower, who has written a memoir of Thompson and other documents that are now a part of the Thompson papers at the Huntington Library.

3. Heather Treseler, "Battles in the Boudoir: Thompson's Intimate Metaphors of War," in *Dunstan Thompson: On the Life and Work of a Lost American Master* (Warrensburg, MO: Pleiades Press, 2010), 111.

4. "Memories of Dunstan Thompson, a letter by Sanford Gifford," in *Dunstan Thompson*, 79.

5. Katie Ford, "'I Can Only Promise Poems': Finding Dunstan Thompson," in *Dunstan Thompson*, 154.

6. Joseph Killorin, ed., *Selected Letters of Conrad Aiken* (New Haven and London: Yale University Press, 1978), 221.

7. Dana Gioia, "Revisiting *Vice Versa*," in *Dunstan Thompson*, 99–107.

8. *Dunstan Thompson*, 6.

9. Katie Ford, "'I Can Only Promise Poems,'" in *Dunstan Thompson*, 155.

10. In his afterword, Dana Gioia considers at greater length the continuity of Thompson's spiritual and theological preoccupations throughout the corpus of his poetry.

Acknowledgments

I am grateful to the many individuals who have helped to bring this collection into being. First and foremost, my thanks go to Dunstan Thompson's longtime companion Philip Trower, who has been a model of graciousness and patience throughout the course of this project. Dana Gioia not only contributed a substantial afterword but has done much—behind the scenes and in the literary public square—to preserve Thompson's literary legacy. Kevin Prufer, who co-edited a volume of essays on Thompson a few years back, was unfailingly kind and helpful with my numerous questions and requests. Paul Mariani provided me with insights into Thompson's literary influences. Mark Jarman and Jerry Harp also offered timely assistance. Jim and Beverly Ohlman once again welcomed me to their beautiful place on Orcas Island so that I could complete the introduction to this book in peace and quiet. Sara Arrigoni did all the initial transcription and copyediting. Julie Mullins, Slant's associate editor, contributed her usual passion for clarity and precision to the final stages of production. Barry Moser brought his inimitable skills as an artist to the creation of a new portrait of Thompson. Jon Stock and Jim Tedrick at Wipf & Stock have gone beyond the call of duty to support Slant Books. Finally, my wife, Suzanne, and our four children surround me with the love in which I live and move and have my being. Thanks to one and all.

—Gregory Wolfe